Prayers on Fire

365 Days Praying the Psalms

Brian Simmons
& Gretchen Rodriguez

BroadStreet
PUBLISHING

BroadStreet Publishing Group, LLC
Savage, Minnesota, USA
BroadStreetPublishing.com

Prayers on Fire: 365 Days Praying the Psalms

Copyright © 2017 The Passion Translation®
Written by Brian Simmons and Gretchen Rodriguez

ISBN 978-1-4245-5389-1 (faux leather)
ISBN 978-1-4245-5390-7 (e-book)

Stock or custom editions of BroadStreet Publishing titles may be
purchased in bulk for educational, business, ministry, fundraising,
or sales promotional use. For information, please e-mail info@
broadstreetpublishing.com.

Cover design by Chris Garborg at garborgdesign.com
Typesetting by Katherine Lloyd at theDESKonline.com

Printed in China or the United States of America
18 19 20 21 5 4 3 2

For almost three thousand years, people have prayed and sung the Psalms. Like those who have gone before us, when we are filled with joy, we will find fuel in these ancient songs for even higher praises. And when we are going through the valley of deepest darkness, we will find in the Psalms light shining upon us, driving the shadows of doubt away. So I encourage you to open your heart as you open the pages of this book. Here you will find God as your Shelter of Strength.

Everything about you was made for God. You were created to need His presence. The true longing of your heart is to know Him, for you were formed in his image (Genesis 1:26–27). Prayer is expressing this soul-thirst for God. We come alive when we come before our True Source. The human spirit is empowered by prayer. Absolutely nothing else compares to being with him!

Prayers on Fire will connect you to God's heart. As you take a portion of your day to pray aloud these devotional prayers (and I do encourage you to pray them out loud), your heart will burn with your soul's desire to connect with the Eternal. Like a deer panting for refreshment, we thirst for the living God—a thirst that can sometimes be overwhelming. We just can't go on without a fresh infilling from the Fountain of Life, and it's prayer and what the Life-Giver does through it that gives us that needed infilling.

Prayer is God's way of drawing us into his heart. He knows that life-changing power is released when we spend time with Jesus in prayer. Adoration turns into transformation—if we will be patient. To love him is our supreme occupation. The more we love him, the more we spend time with him. And the more we spend time with him, the more our soul is transformed into his image (2 Corinthians 3:18; John 14:21). As we give him our heart in prayer, he gives us his heart in exchange, transforming us deep within. *God will change you through prayer.*

This book is filled with adventure! It will take you through the poetry and prayers of the Psalms over the course of one year. Make it your goal to read it through cover to cover. If you miss a day, the chapters are short enough for you to catch up. We are praying for you that as you go through *Prayers on Fire,* your life will soar with fresh courage and tender devotion to Christ. Are you ready for that adventure?

Brian Simmons
The Passion Translation Project

January

Imminent

O God-Enthroned in heaven,
I worship and adore you!
Psalm 123:1

God, you are enthroned upon my heart. I'm consumed with desire—a longing to touch what is unseen, yet real. So incredibly real. You are the profound truth that guides me and purifies my motives. You absorb my failings and grant me unending mercy. You are love.

When you speak, my heart comes alive. When you whisper, my soul finds peace. You are the breath that pushes me forward. The grace I discover each day.

There's a fire burning deep within, ignited by your touch. I want to know you. To honor you. To please you with a life of unrelenting devotion. I want to discover the secrets that you've hidden for me to find. I want to be pure in heart. I want to see you. This beating in my chest tells me it's not too late. You are imminent. You are near.

My Greatest Treasure

*I find more joy in following what you tell me to do
than in chasing after all the wealth of the world!*
Psalm 119:14

There is so much power that comes from walking in your truth. Abiding in your Word is the path to wisdom and purity. It is the only way I know to steer through the labyrinth of life. It is the light that guides my steps and the voice that speaks louder than my fears. It comforts me and kisses me with freedom. It is the strongest weapon in my arsenal—the power of your Spirit upon my lips.

Never let me stray from your commandments. I will write them upon my heart and meditate upon them even as I sleep. Counsel me with your precepts and keep me close to you, so that I won't sin against you. Wonderful God, I praise you above all else! Teach me the power of your decrees and reveal the mysteries of your prophecies. Your words are my greatest treasure and following them is life's greatest delight.

Yahweh

Be in awe before his majesty.
Be in awe before such power and might!
Come worship wonderful Yahweh arrayed in all his splendor,
bowing in worship as he appears in all his holy beauty.

Psalm 29:2

God, you are arrayed in splendor. You rule with majesty and holiness, eternity at your side. You are stunning—radiant and glorious. Struck with awe, I can do nothing more than bow low and worship you.

I hear a symphony playing as nature sings your song; the clashing of symbols as the waters break against the shore. The power of your voice splinters the mighty forests and echoes through the sky. It shakes the deserts, yet speaks to me with tender care. Stars sparkle as they dance on the edge of your fingertips, while the oceans reveal the depths of your love.

You are the strength of storms, the roar of thunder, the flashes of lightning, and the rush of wind. Though your eyes blaze with fire and tempt me to cower and hide, I cannot look away. Consuming me again with holy passion, you draw me in.

I fall prostrate before you in awe and wonder. You strengthen me, and it is only by your grace that I may stand before someone so holy. You kiss me with peace and call me your child. You lift me up and call me your friend.

The Place of Wonder

Listen to me all you godly ones:
Love the Lord with passion!
The Lord protects and preserves
all those who are loyal to him.

Psalm 31:23

I open my eyes to find myself standing in the beautiful expanse of answered prayer. This is the place of freedom, where dreams come true. You illuminate the dark places with the radiant splendor of your face. You lavish your undying love upon me until I can barely speak.

Yes, this is the place of reverent wonder. Where I'm struck silent—amazed at your faithfulness; humbled by my lack of patience while I waited for you. Forgive me for thinking you deserted me.

Tears of love soak my face as I ponder how wonderful you are. You've come through once again. All you require is a sincere heart that loves you—a radiant lover who honors you and worships you, even in the hardest of times. To this one, you pour out blessings that astound us. You surprise us with treasure that you've been storing up all along.

Lord, I pray for those who are as weary as I was—strengthen them with courage, overshadow them with your glorious presence as they wait for you.

I am Yours

You took me in and made me yours.
Now teach me all about your ways and tell me what to do.
Make it clear for me to understand.
Psalm 27:10–11

You have made me yours. You answered my passionate cry for mercy and have become my strength. You cherish me. You love me. You will never let me fall. I am chosen.

All of my days I will sing of your goodness and undeserved favor. How wonderfully you care for me—like a father doting over a precious child. You teach me your ways and illuminate my journey with perfect wisdom.

Every longing in my heart ultimately leads to you. You are the fulfillment of every dream—the healing for every pain. You are life and love. You are perfect deliverance. You have removed hypocrisy from my heart and clothed me with righteousness. I choose the humble posture of love. I clothe myself in praise. I am yours.

Just Breathe

Surrender your anxiety!
Be silent and stop your striving
and you will see that I am God.
Psalm 46:10

Breathe. That's all I can do. I've done everything else. I've prayed every prayer, I've sung every song, and I've cried every tear. I can't fix these things that spin out of control. I'm exhausted. God, I don't know what to do.

You are silent. I know that you're close, but the only sound I hear is the chaos raging inside of me. Speak to me. Let the fire of your love burn away everything that is not of you.

Gently you come. I feel the faint touch of your Spirit—a wisp of light in the midst of darkness. Embrace me. Let me lean into your presence.

I hear you now—whispering truths that begin to chase away my fears. You tell me to be still, to release my cares to you, so you can step in. In truth, I wonder if I can—anxiety is eating me away. But in obedience, I surrender. Take it, Lord. Take it all. I choose to trust you.

I don't know how long I stay in this holy place before the dawn of hope alights upon my heart, but eventually it does. I am still. My heart is at peace. You are God and you will not forget your promises to me. I love you.

To Laugh Again

Lord God, unlock my heart, unlock my lips,
and I will overcome with my joyous praise!
Psalm 51:15

Sometimes I feel stuck, the cares of life gluing me within a cocoon of melancholy that I cannot escape. There is only one solution and you are it. I want to soar with you and feel the intoxicating delight of freedom once again.

Fan away the gloomy clouds of heaviness and unclutter my mind. Catch the little foxes hidden deep within my heart and untangle my soul from anxiety. Come, take my hand and together we'll dance away my cares.

I can't help but smile when I feel you near. You cause the stars to shine and my heart to sing. When I'm with you, I'm alive—raptured by pleasures few have ever known. Your presence unlocks the treasures of joy within me. You breathe wonder and delight into my soul, so I can laugh again!

You Have Restored My Roar

Through your glorious name and your awesome power
we can push through to any victory and defeat every enemy.

Psalm 44:5

God, you are faithful. Nothing can stand in my way! You are my Champion who has overcome. When you filled me with your power, you equipped me to be just like you. When you put your words in my heart, you gave me a sword to wield. My posture will not be one of defeat or fear, for you have given me the victory!

Just standing in your presence infuses me with faith. I will run through the fires and dance in the storms. Your radiant presence burns through the camp of the enemy, destroying the wickedness that opposes you.

When hopelessness tries to steal my joy, I will not relent. I will stare fear in the face, for you have restored my roar. Your strength has saved me.

When I'm Overwhelmed

I'm slipping away and on the verge of a breakdown,
with nothing but sorrow and sighing.

Psalm 38:17

I'm bowed before your throne. In need of your mercy once again. I come just as I am—an imperfect vessel filled with a perfect God. I won't cower in fear from your righteous gaze. I know you see everything. My heart and mind are at odds and I need you.

I can't survive this world without you. The demands of life are too much for me. It seems everything is fighting for my attention. I'm on the verge of a breakdown and it's my own fault. I've let people pull me in every direction, schedules dictate my peace, and the chaos looming in the distance fills me with fear. I'm not sure how I ever lost sight of you. Forgive me!

I can't hold it in any longer. Without you, I'm a mess. I need to experience you again. To bask in the reality of your love. I choose to stay here and hide myself in you, until these distractions disappear. I want to worship you until nothing else matters. Come with your mercy, free me with your love.

Suffering in Silence

Please deal gently with me;
show me mercy for I'm sick and frail.
I'm fading away with weakness.
Heal me, for I'm falling apart.

Psalm 6:2

Lord, show me how to love those who are hurting and suffering in silence. Teach me to be patient with those who pull away and retreat. Show me how I can help them.

So many times you have come to my rescue. You have lifted me out of the pit of despair and caused me to laugh again. Now I'm asking for you to do the same for those around me who feel as if they are falling apart. Reach out in ways only you know how and ignite their hearts with hope. Heal the wounds and disappointments that cause them pain. Restore them and redeem their past. Shine the light of your glory into their darkest hour.

When I'm with them, fill me with wisdom and compassion, and teach me how to love. Give me ideas and creative ways to be a blessing to them. Show me how to make them feel valued and understood. Help me to empower them, so they find the courage to let go of the pain. Let my joy be contagious. Set them free!

Deeply Rooted

They will be standing firm like a flourishing tree
planted by God's design,
deeply rooted by the brooks of bliss;
bearing fruit in every season of their lives.
They are never dry, never fainting,
ever blessed, ever prosperous.

Psalm 1:3

Lord, I immerse myself in the depths of your light. Reveal what is true and right. I allow myself to sink beyond the mire of worldly consummations, to find truth by walking with you. Each thought turns into musings of your unfailing love.

Moment by moment I discover the joys of walking on the path you have set before me. You are my sure footing, the One who sustains me. Let me ever remain true—rooted deeply in your love, saturated with the waters of your pleasure, constantly aware of your nearness.

Life with you satisfies the deepest yearnings of my soul. In you I flourish, bearing fruit in every season. In this place of unrelenting devotion, I will never be dry; could never be disappointed, because you are here with me.

Every fiber of my being overflows with joy and wonder. You faithfully watch over the paths of those who love you, leading them on a sacred journey with you.

My Source

*Many blessings are waiting for all
who turn aside to hide themselves in him!*

Psalm 2:12

From the depths of my heart, I worship, knowing I am covered and protected by your presence. You've brought me close—right into the brilliance of your glory. Your arms are a shield that cannot be penetrated by the sharpest of arrows. Your embrace is like a lullaby and I sleep soundly, knowing I'll awake in the place of safety and bliss.

In you, I am truly alive. As I hide myself within your greatness, I discover your eternal purposes. You are my awe-inspiring God—in love and humility I bow. The way you watch over me infuses me with confidence and courage. I find I can stand on my own two feet again because you are with me.

You are my Source; I draw life from the waters of your love. Walking step-by-step with you brings me joy unlike that I've ever known. Your Word illuminates my path and wherever we go, I flourish. No matter the season, I'm blessed—established firmly in you.

Stronger than Before

Yes, they surrounded me,
like a swarm of killer bees swirling around me.
I was trapped like one trapped by a raging fire;
I was surrounded with no way out and at the point of collapse.
But by Yahweh's supernatural power I overcame them all!

Psalm 118:11–12

When my enemy surrounds me like a swarm of bees, you are there. When someone who was once a trusted confidant, betrays me, bad-mouths me, and pushes me to the edge, you pick me up and heal my wounds. Your compassion is unlike any other. You know what it's like to suffer rejection. The difference is that you suffered it for me.

Together we have overcome. You have helped me through many difficult times and I'm so thankful. You are my true strength, my glory-song, my Champion, and my Savior! You never fail me. I will never again fear what mere mortals can do to me.

I'm stronger than before, because of your love. Not only has joy and gladness returned to my heart, but I see those who hurt me through new lenses. I see them with your heart. Lord, extend your tender mercy and teach them your ways. Draw them to you, the way you did with me. You alone have the power to lift heavy shadows from darkened hearts.

Revive Me

Lord, I'm fading away. I'm discouraged
and lying in the dust;
revive me by your Word,
just like you promised you would!
Psalm 119:25

Lord, I'm so discouraged. I feel as if I'm at the breaking point. I've poured my life into serving you, but lately nothing seems to be going right. It's as if everything I do backfires. Help me not to make a mess of things. Hold me close so I don't sin against you by throwing away my faith.

Revive me with the words that stream from your heart. Open up my understanding, so I will see things from your point of view. Keep me far away from what is false—leaning on my own understanding or putting confidence in the opinions of those who don't care anything about you.

I need grace to stay true and continue running after you. For now, I will rest in your presence and let your Spirit strengthen me. Lord, the same way that the enemy had nothing in you that belonged to him, I want nothing in me that doesn't reflect you. Take me deeper into your perfect love. I choose to trust you.

Magnificent

I bow down before your divine presence
and bring you my deepest worship
as I experience your tender love and your living truth.
For the promises of your Word and the fame of your name
have been magnified above all else!

Psalm 138:2

Lord, I come before you with a humble heart. How great you are! How magnificent! In the presence of angels, I bow down before your holy presence and adore you. There is none like you—none whose truth shakes the heavens.

Though you are more glorious than all the kings of the earth, you stoop to embrace the lowly and acquaint yourself with the suffering of humanity. Your wonderful ways are celebrated by all who discover them. Your promises are yes and amen. The fame of your name will one day bring the nations to their knees in reverence.

With deepest affection, I offer you my tears of thanksgiving and joy. You know me—every thought, every deed, every fear, and every hope—and yet you believe in me. I surrender everything to you. All I ask is that you would finish what you've started in me, so I will become what you already see.

Love

But as for me, your strength shall be my song of joy.
At each and every sunrise, my lyrics of your love will fill the air!
Psalm 59:16

I've become obsessed with this one truth—God, you love me. What a wonderful revelation! Each morning, when I wake and turn my heart to you, let that be my first thought. Let it fill my soul with hope and flood every cell with joy. Knowing you love me changes everything. The Creator of the universe, the One who made it all, loves me!

I want everything I do to flow from this posture of complete confidence in your love. I want to pursue this love forever—to worship you and you alone. Let love be the motivation for my life. Throughout the day, regardless of the challenges I face, let your love be my constant meditation. It is the provision for every situation.

I will trust in this love without reservation, believing in your promises. Such freedom in your love! Such peace to be found within it.

Nothing can ever separate me from this love. How amazing it is to be your child! May the power of your love set the course for my life.

Faith

Honor me by trusting in me in your day of trouble.
Cry aloud to me, and I will be there to rescue you.
That is what I desire from you!

Psalm 50:15

Lord, teach me to rest. I relinquish my cares, my worries, my anxieties to you. Free me from these limitations of unbelief. Release my soul from the entanglements of fear, so I will no longer be a victim of its torment.

I choose to believe you are the God of restoration. You will use these difficult times to springboard me into something beautiful and amazing. Though I sometimes feel disoriented in this maze of life, you restore my sense of direction. Nothing is too hard for you.

May the desires of my heart honor you. Let faith give me eyes that see. Unite my heart and mind, so my words create substance for me to walk upon. May the mountains of doubt move at my command. Lean in, Lord, hear my cry, and come to my rescue.

I will wait. I will trust. I will believe.

Holy Devotion

*Lord, I will offer myself freely, and everything I am I give to you.
I will worship and praise your name, O Lord,
for it is precious to me.*

Psalm 54:6

Lord, unite my will to yours. Spirit, soul, and body—I consecrate myself to you and depend upon your grace. Let me be so fully devoted to you that nothing will ever turn my heart away. Remove the barriers I have unknowingly created. Burn away everything that is contrary to your Holy Spirit.

I want every moment of my life to revolve around loving you. Whether in worship or in my daily tasks, guide me into a lifestyle of adoration. I want to be continually aware of you—the beginning and end of all I think and do. No matter what is happening around me, may I be eternally drawn to your presence.

In you I lack nothing. Your very name is power and majesty. Your presence is peace, joy, and full provision for every situation. I want to experience the fullness of your love. To worship you in spirit and truth—with unrelenting, unyielding devotion. May everything I do flow from a heart of pure and holy devotion. I give you the pleasing offering of my life.

Quiet Confidence

You are my Satisfaction, Lord, and all that I need;
so I'm determined to do everything you say.

Psalm 119:57

You are my satisfaction. From abstract chaos you build floors for me to dance upon. Your nearness floods my soul with peace that silences every fear. My thoughts are focused and clear when I choose to stay my mind on you. Everywhere I look, I see your love and tender care.

When temptation encircles me with evil, I remember you—my strength, my hope, the One who is more than enough. Your grace makes it easy to walk away. I want nothing to hinder me from this place of purity I've found in you. Reveal the glory of your ways, so I will never stray.

You are the peace found in every moment. The stillness of my soul. Even in the middle of the night, I wake and feel you near. Unveil my eyes to see you more clearly. Free me even more to live in this place of serenity, where every thought leads to you. Where joyful trust releases my soul.

Light of the World

How glad the nations will be when you are their King.
They will sing, they will shout, for you
give true justice to the people.
Yes! You, Lord, are the Shepherd of the nations!

Psalm 67:4

God, you are the light of the world. Shine your radiant smile on me, so that as I travel the globe, people will be drawn to the splendor of your glory. May your grace stream like a free-flowing fountain over my life, spilling to those around me. As I love and enjoy you, let my excitement become contagious, so others will discover you are in their midst.

Once they see that you rule with dignity and honor, they will burst forth with praise. The earth needs a true king. You Lord, are that King. How amazing it will be when you are invited into every nation, tribe, and culture. You will finally give us the justice we have needed. You will do more than rule us, you will shepherd us with a Father's heart.

When everyone finally gives you the honor you deserve, the earth will be filled with glory. Our praise of you will never cease and you will bless our lands. Reveal your love, so even the hardest of hearts may come to know you.

Near

How satisfied we will be just to be near you!
Psalm 65:4

What an incomprehensible joy it is to know you and be known by you! I don't have the words to adequately express your worth, so I stand in silence, my heart filled with praise. Simply being near you is exhilarating—satisfying the deepest longings of my soul. Though my sins should separate me from you, you have brought me near through your perfect sacrifice and call me your friend. How kind you are. How merciful.

I don't think I will ever understand the favor you've shown me. Nor will I ever comprehend this unrestrained love that knows no end. You invite me into your sanctuary and give me a seat at your table; I feast on your mercy.

Your love is on display through mighty wonders and jaw-dropping power. The entire world looks to you. Thank you for caring for us like a Father, while ruling as a righteous God. You are the desire of the nations. Our hope is in you.

Examine My Heart

God, I invite your searching gaze into my heart.
Examine me through and through;
find out everything that may be hidden within me.
Put me to the test and sift through all my anxious cares.

Psalm 139:23

Father, I fall prostrate before your holy presence. I surrender all that I am to you and give you full control of my life. There is nothing I want more than to become a vessel of pure devotion and to live each day consumed in this glorious love. Come, examine my heart and reveal anything that would distance me from you.

The nearness of your Spirit is like fire in my bones, sifting through every part of me. I will not resist. You know my weaknesses, yet you chose to dwell within my frailty. I stand humbled by your beauty, amazed by your power and grace.

As I meditate upon your Word, I feel it working within me, peeling away layers of darkness I didn't know were there. With the precision of a surgeon's knife, it cuts away the hidden cares.

Have your way in me, Lord. I trust you. Cleanse me from secret sins and purify my heart.

Running after You

I will run after you with delight in my heart.
Psalm 119:32

Your presence is alive! I'm running after you like a child chasing a father who longs to be caught. I'm free! Hold me. Dance with me. Let's run through the open fields of your glory. Together, we'll sing our songs of jubilee.

Your love fills me with joy. Just when I thought life couldn't get any better, you prove me wrong. You love to surprise me. The depth of your Spirit calls to the depth of my soul, and I respond with full surrender. Nothing means more to me than being here with you.

God, you are the fountain of life. There's always more to see and know when I walk with you. Open my eyes to partake of all that you want to show me. Pierce my heart with revelation truth. Take me from glory to glory. My soul delights in you.

Find Me

I'm sinking into the mud with no place to stand,
and I'm about to drown in this storm.

Psalm 69:2

Lord, I'm stuck. I'm sinking deeper and deeper into the mud, and I can't get out. I don't even know how to pray any more. It feels as if I've prayed every prayer I can pray and quoted every Scripture I know.

I've lost momentum. I've allowed the cares of this world and the busyness of life to drown me. Instead of running to you, I run in circles, trying to get everything else done. Schedules dictate my life. I need a break. I need you.

Give me a fresh start. Chase away the dark clouds that fill my head. Pull me out of this rut. Forgive me for letting my priorities get out of line, even for a moment. I'm at a loss for words and that's okay. There are only three words that matter: *I love you.*

When I'm overwhelmed and cannot seem to find your presence, I will sit and worship. In the stillness, you will find me.

Mystery

Without a sound, without a word,
without a voice being heard,
Yet all the world can see its story.
Everywhere its gospel is clearly read so all may know.
Psalm 19:3–4

Lord, I hear you even when you don't say a word. I feel you as you rise within me. Your presence is unmistakable. Your glory is a mystery I long to unravel.

You are grace and light, power and might. You are the first and the last. You are the question everyone asks and the answer too many refuse to accept. To me you are Savior, Father, and Friend. You are the beauty that lives inside of me and the One who gave me joy when you saved my soul. I will not wrestle with truth, simply because it is too high for me to understand.

You are immortal and eternal—you always were and always will be. YHWH—men cannot pronounce your name. I am crucified with you, yet seated with you in heavenly places. You are near and far—present with me, yet also with others. My mind cannot grasp such things, so I will embrace them with my heart.

In Sorrow

Even when their path winds through the dark valley of tears,
they dig deep to find a pleasant pool where others find only pain.
He gives to them a brook of blessing
filled from the rain of an outpouring.

Psalm 84:6

Lord, thank you for allowing me to go through the difficult seasons. There was a time in my life when I never thought I would say those words, but now I look back and see how glorious those dark times really were.

In the midst of my deepest pain, I learned how immediate and tangible your presence can be. You pour out such tender love and comfort when I need you the most. Had I not gone through those moments, seeking you in the midst of them, I would not have known the beauty of your consolation.

When my whole world is falling apart, you come as a loving Father and hold me in your arms. With whispers of hope, you always strengthen me. You remind me of your promises and your never failing truth. You reach into my deepest pain and heal it with your love.

Though I don't enjoy the seasons of sorrow, I'm so grateful for the many things I've learned. I praise you for being present with me and manifesting your love so faithfully.

Fierce Protector

Your perfection and faithfulness are my bodyguards,
for you are my hope and I trust in you as my only protection.

Psalm 25:21

Come closer, Lord. Even closer. You are the only One who can save me from this slimy pit of despair. These trials are more than I can handle. It feels like things have gone from bad to worse. Though I've trusted you over and over again, every so often I need you to surround me like a bodyguard and rescue me.

You are my Fierce Protector. You have ransomed me with the price of blood, and I will not dishonor you by doubting your love. It is only when I surrender my fears and receive your promises that I remember how near you are. I fix my eyes on you.

Though trouble surrounds me, your faithfulness scoops me up and brings me near. Redeemer, you are my only hope. Let me be known as an unwavering lover of God. One who gazes upon your face and trusts you even when I feel alone and confused. My soul prospers as I hide myself in you.

The Awe of Knowing You

Who, then, ascends into the presence of the Lord?
And who has the privilege of entering into God's Holy Place?

Psalm 24:3

Father, I can't stop thinking about how powerful you are. How creative you are. How majestic. You created the whole world and everything in it. As an artist paints with brushstrokes upon a canvas, you pushed back the oceans where you wanted to see dry land.

The entire universe moves in rhythmic harmony, a beautiful symphony led by the most skilled conductor. Every flower, every tree, every creature—every human being—exists because of you. Each intricate detail designed by your wisdom.

I am amazed that someone like me is welcomed into the presence of someone like you. I'm struck with wonder at the privilege of entering the Most Holy Place. The pleasure of gazing upon your face is more glorious than life itself.

Let me never get used to this. May I always feel the awe of standing before my Savior and King. May my heart always be true. May I remain clean—my works, ways, and motives always pure. I long to forever hear the sounds of life that flow from your heart as I lean upon your chest. May I remain forever yours.

Misplaced Affection

Dead men can only create dead idols.
And everyone who trusts in these powerless, dead things
will be just like what they worship—powerless and dead!
Psalm 115:8

How easily we ignore you and turn to frivolous things. How often we live by what stimulates the senses with immediate gratification, instead of patiently searching for truth. You are a treasure waiting to be excavated and enjoyed—hidden as a gift for all humankind. Instead, many idolize what they own, as if it will bring life and meaning to their souls.

Have mercy on the spiritually blind, Lord, they can only create blind things. Those who are dead can only reproduce death. Grasp their hands, lead them from their paths that lead to destruction. Those who worship their wealth and work have lost sight of you. They don't realize how powerless and dead they truly are.

Your beauty is without compare. Your presence, a magnificent shield wrapped around those whose heart is set upon you. Forgive the futility of misplaced affections and neglected faith. Though we grasp for substance, we satisfy ourselves with junk.

Hidden Treasure

Everything you speak to me is like joyous treasure,
filling my life with gladness.
Psalm 119:111

Everything you say to me is like discovering the jewels of a hidden, sacred treasure. They make me beautiful and sparkle with hidden mystery. They are bountiful provision, which can feed a multitude. Fill my life with the joy of uncovering your cherished truths, which guide my choices and make my paths clear.

Your truth is the source of my understanding. It is my holy and lifelong commitment. I am determined to obey you, fully and forever. Teach me how to please you even more, for I've found that following you is the fountain of inexhaustible happiness.

Strengthen my inner being with the promises of your Word. Lift me up and wrap me in your never-ending love. You are my place of quiet retreat. Every time I meditate on these gems of truths, I'm encouraged. Hold me close, so I will experience every moment of life with you.

Reflect

*I lie awake each night thinking of you
and reflecting on how you help me like a Father.*
Psalm 63:6

When the night falls, I lie in bed and reflect on your never-ceasing help. Your tender care is seen in every living thing. I sense your nearness as I gaze upon the stars, which you set in place. I see your artistry in every rainbow and feel your glory in every sun-drenched sky.

The earth boasts your creativity. Even the birds sing your song. I stare with the awestruck wonder of a child, at this One I call Father. My heart swells with admiration—you're my Hero.

Under your splendor-shadow I sing songs of love throughout the night. As my head rests upon my pillow, I imagine lying safely upon your chest, snuggled up in the arms of my Father-God. Your strong hands steady me day by day. You draw me near, and with passionate pursuit I will run after you and never let you go.

February

Not Abandoned

You are my Savior and I'm always in your thoughts.
So don't delay to deliver me now, for you are my God.

Psalm 70:5

God, I will praise you in the midst of brokenness. When everyone—friends, family, and even my leaders—abandons me, I will look to you. My life is an open book; you know I've done nothing to deserve this. All I've done is pursued you with passion. Yet they treat me with contempt, just as they did you.

It's in these times, when I'm exhausted and discouraged, that my praise means the most to you. I won't stop trusting you. I won't stop crying out for you. You *will* come and rescue me. You know what I'm going through. Your compassion, grace, and constant love are never held back from me—even when I don't feel it. I'm always in your thoughts.

My sincere worship means more to you than any gift or sacrifice. As I keep my heart humble, you'll not only pull me out of this pit, you'll lift me to the highest place to be near you. You won't abandon me. You'll revive my heart and flood it with peace and joy. I will rejoice in you, my Savior, and tell the world how great and glorious you are.

See Again

You're a proven help in time of trouble—
more than enough and always available whenever I need you.
Psalm 46:1

Sometimes your presence greets me swiftly and profoundly. At other times it feels as though I am running through mud just to get to you. The truth is that even when you seem to be a million miles away, you are always here—the Eternal Now.

Come and silence the noise within. I turn my thoughts to you. Still the storms that play in my mind. I've searched for a way out of this, but the truth is, you are the Way. You've proven your faithfulness. I don't know why I would ever doubt. Instead, I will trust you, taking this moment to love you, worship you, and be thankful.

You are always ready to create hope when I am hopeless. You reveal the passion inside of me that stirs me to greater things. You are more than enough. Thank you for being so patient with me. Thank you for breathing faith into my heart, so I can see again. I glorify you!

Liquid Love

You anoint me with the fragrance of your Holy Spirit;
you give me all I can drink of you until my heart overflows.
Psalm 23:5

Lord, I love your presence. As I look back upon the seasons of my life, I find your fingerprints everywhere. The beauty of your fellowship sustains me. Faithfully you draw me, day after day, into the garden of your love.

Anoint me with the oil of your Holy Spirit. Let it saturate me until every cell in my body is dripping with the fragrance of your love. Transform me from the inside out. I want to smell like you and look like you, leaving the impact of your glory everywhere I go.

Your words are like liquid love. They flood my senses and awaken my heart. I drink them until I am overflowing with grace and truth. They have become a part of me, dwelling within my frailty. Let me drink constantly of the reality of this truth. I'm lovesick, ruined for anything else.

The Path to Your Presence

Remember this: the Righteous Lord loves
what is right and just, and every godly one
will come into his presence and gaze upon his face!

Psalm 11:7

I want to see your face. To gaze into the eyes that have inflamed my heart with holy passion. You are the object of my desire. Draw me closer.

Lord, I've consecrated myself to you and seek to walk the narrow way of righteousness. The veil has been torn and you call me your own, but I long to know you more. I yearn for unclouded vision. I earnestly desire to touch you; to reach out and hold the hand that so often holds mine.

Impart to me the gift of compassion that I may love the way you love and forgive the way you forgive. I want my words to mirror your heart and reveal motives that are pure. Restrain my mind from wandering thoughts. I want to live a life that pleases you, so nothing I do will hinder me on the path that leads to your presence.

Vision

*All your lovers will be pleased
because the future belongs to them.*
Psalm 94:15

Unlock destiny within me. Without a vision, I will perish! I feel things stirring inside of me, but I need you to bring clarity and life to each hazy idea. Impregnate me with desires that will launch me forward and bring you glory. Help me to see the potential I have for greater things. I want to discover your purpose for my life.

Fill me with faith, hope, and dreams. Let me see the endless possibilities I've yet to discover. Open doors for me, so I can see which way to go. I lean into your wisdom and incline my heart to understand. Give me downloads from heaven. I will boldly step into all you have for me.

Each day I will seek your face, knowing you will bless me. Reveal the specific promises you have for my life, as you did for Abraham when you told him his descendants would be as numerous as the stars in the sky. Give me a vision to hold onto and we will walk it out together. Cover me with favor as I move into the unknown.

Happy

Shine and make your joyful boast in him, you lovers of God.
Let's be happy and keep rejoicing no matter what.

Psalm 105:3

I choose to be happy and to believe the best! Life can be overwhelming at times, but I refuse to let it steal my joy. My happiness comes when I look to you and release every care. When I find the smile on your face and hear you laughing at your enemies, I am filled with hope.

You are the only one who can make me truly happy. I will not look to others to fill a void that only you can fill. Each day I will wake up and tap into you—the only source of true joy and unlimited freedom. Your ways are perfect. You have nothing but the best in store for me. And you created me for an amazing life.

Even when things are difficult and I go through the lowest valley, I set my mind on you and you fill me with peace. Just like you, I can laugh and be happy, no matter what I face. Let your kingdom—righteousness, peace, and joy—manifest in my life!

Unaware

Such amazing mysteries found within every miracle
that nearly everyone seems to miss.
Those with no discernment can never really discover
the deep and glorious secrets hidden in your ways!
Psalm 92:6

There is no beginning or end to your love. You're ever present—with me, even when I'm unaware. You save me from danger I can't see. You whisper wisdom's words, leading me as I go about my day. And you're faithful—caring for me constantly.

Teach me to look for you in every moment: in laughter, tears, and the mundane tasks of life. I want to discover you in everything and hear what you have to say. You're continually drawing me into the awareness of your presence, waiting for me to respond.

Your ways are so amazing. Thank you for being with me. May I never become so accustomed to the way you love me that I forget that every day is a gift. You have blessed me with yourself.

Rescuer

His love broke open the way
and he brought me into a beautiful broad place.
He rescued me—because his delight is in me!

Psalm 18:19

You never stop running after me. Your love broke open the way to the promises you've made. Every one of them are faithful and true. Now I see the light that everyone said was at the end of this tunnel and it floods my soul with wonder. You've come just as you said you would. Your love found me buried beneath the dust of my own fears and you lifted me up in a hurricane of grace.

The storms that were meant to take me out thundered your voice when you called my name. You breathed life into me again. Now I'm dancing through the desert to get to the Promised Land.

My tears of thankfulness and joy become more than sweet release, they become a gift of worship. I will embrace them, the same way I cradled the tears of pain. Let them wash my soul and bring you delight. Thank you for all you've done. You are my Rescuer.

Climb

May you be pleased with every sweet thought
I have about you, for you are
the source of my joy and gladness!

Psalm 104:34

You are my pure and holy obsession. I want to see you. I will climb above the distractions of lowly thinking and turn my thoughts to you. Higher into your presence you will take me. You are the source of my joy and the strength of my life. Show me your glory.

The more I lean into you and trust your love for me, the more of you I experience. I've never deserved your love and I still don't—nothing I could ever do would make me worthy enough. Yet without conditions, you lavish your affection upon me and call me your own.

Lord, when I come into your presence, help me to rest. To soak up your unconditional love and turn off my racing mind. The sweetness of your touch revives me. The movement of your Spirit unlocks my heart and sets me free. You transform me in ways I never knew were possible. I am fully yours.

Listening

God-lovers make the best counselors.
Their words possess wisdom and are right and trustworthy.
Psalm 37:30

Lord, teach me how to be there for others, the way you're there for me. When friends and acquaintances come to me for advice, or simply need a listening ear, help me to bless them with what their hearts truly need.

Let patience and compassion set the tone. Anoint me as I lead them into your presence and engage with them heart to heart. Give me wisdom to help them find the answers only you hold. Help me to listen, so they feel valued and understood.

You have equipped me to be an encouragement to those around me and to teach them to care for the garden of their hearts. Your Spirit is at work within me to set others free. Teach me how to correctly respond to their brokenness, always focusing on the answers and not the problems. I want to be a vessel of your love, leading others to become the powerful people you created them to be.

Eternal Wisdom

Lord, you will reign forever!
Zion's God will rule throughout time and eternity!
Hallelujah! Praise the Lord!
Psalm 146:10

What a joyful thing it is to behold your wisdom. It is seen throughout time and eternity—when oceans slept in the palm of your hand, and humanity was yet a desire in your heart. By it you reign forever in perfected authority.

With the voice of wisdom, you spoke a word and created light, which still heeds your command. Your promises are never failing and full of power. Even death yields to your edict of life. There is nothing you can't do!

These same words of wisdom speak peace to my troubled soul, bringing joy and delight in the place of heartache and fear. Though the counsel of the godly can steer me in the right direction, only you can guide me into perfect truth. Even the greatest leaders are merely human, offering wisdom that merely grazes the edges of your understanding.

God, I honor your wisdom and place my trust in you.

Surrendered

*Help me turn my eyes away from illusions
so that I pursue only that which is true;
drench my soul with life as I walk in your paths.*

Psalm 119:37

I bow in humility before your great wisdom. I long for every facet of you. Ignite my heart with the Spirit of desire. Guide me along paths of grace, as I follow what is true. Turn my eyes away from illusions that tempt and seduce. I am your beloved—your servant who bows before you.

I am zealous to know you more. To experience the freedom of limitless faith and soar with you upon the clouds. Give me revelation to understand the mystery of your ways and understanding, so I will follow your truth with passion. Revive my soul with your beautiful words and set my heart ablaze.

My life has become your garden. Your love blossoms in the deserts of weary souls. Smother me with your holy kisses, for your perfect love removes my fear.

Lovely

"I delight to fulfill your will, my God,
for your living words are written upon the pages of my heart."
Psalm 40:8

I'm in awe of you; totally bewildered by your undeserved, unrestrained love. It surges from your throne and crashes through my soul. Blessing after blessing cascades over my heart—you never hold back, because I'm wholeheartedly yours. I'm head-over-heels in love with you, Lord. Though miracles and wonders are found within you, still you take time for me and think of me continually.

Now I willingly say, "Here I am! Your servant for life." It's not sacrifices or offerings that really move your heart. There's nothing I can do that would make you love me more. Instead, I bow low and rest in your love and tremble at the loveliness of your voice. I have no interest in listening to prideful people who brag about all they've done for you, as if their efforts have cleansed them from sin.

Inscribe the pages of my heart with your living words, so I may forever delight in doing your will.

Beautiful

As the princess-bride enters the palace,
how glorious she appears within the holy chamber,
robed with a wedding dress embroidered with pure gold!
Psalm 45:13

Beautiful King, I am in awe of who I've become. Once defined by a cloak of carnal pleasures, I am now dressed in royal garments. Love brought me here—moved my feet and stood me before your very presence.

Though I was dirty and stained by worldly passions, you welcomed me with open arms and invited me before your throne. You dug up the roots of my past and burned them in an inferno of holy love. I'm no longer haunted by what lies behind. Love has transformed me.

The closer I get, the more radiant I become—the spotless bride you've always believed me to be. Each day I discover the gold you have hidden within me—treasures of beauty that flowed from a wooden cross. I am beautiful because you loved me.

Favor

But I keep calling out to you, Lord!
I know you will bend down to listen to me,
for now is the season of favor.

Psalm 69:13

People think I'm lucky, but it's really just your favor upon my life. It surrounds me like a shield everywhere I go. I haven't done anything to deserve it, it's simply a gift. You approve of me, because my heart is toward you. Though I'm far from perfect, you delight in me.

Your favor is better than all the riches in the world because it opens doors of opportunity with people who normally wouldn't give me the time of day. It reaches across every border and draws people to me, creating outlets for the desires of my heart. People listen to me, all because of your hand of blessing upon my life.

I have such favor with you, that you gave me the keys to the kingdom. Whatever things I ask in Jesus' name, I receive. The covenant I have with you gives me entrance into your very presence. You wrap your arms around me and call me friend. You love me so much that you've tattooed my name in the palm of your hand. I will live in this favor forever!

Redeem the Past

Now listen, daughter, pay attention, and forget about your past.
Put behind you every attachment to the familiar,
even those who once were close to you!

Psalm 45:10

God, thank you for the many ways you redeem my past. I am not defined by the traumas that have afflicted me. I choose to move forward. I believe that you are able to heal every memory.

Teach me how to deal with tormenting thoughts, even the seemingly insignificant ones that rise from my subconscious. I will not ignore them. Instead, I will offer them up to you and declare your life-giving words over each one. As I take every imagination captive and submit them to you, memories of pain lose the power of their nagging jabs. Fears will no longer dominate my thinking.

Disappointments don't characterize who I am or what the future holds. Regardless of circumstances or people who have hurt me, your grace leads me forth with joy. Lord, take the lies that have created unhealthy thought patterns and replace them with your truth. Rewire the way I think. What once held me back will catapult me forward into the beautiful life you've created me for.

Sweet Sleep

I can lay down in peace and sleep comes at once,
for no matter what happens, I will live unafraid!

Psalm 4:8

Lord, bless my sleep. From the moment I curl up in bed, fill my heart with peace and my mind with pleasant thoughts. I release the cares of today and the concerns for tomorrow. Spirit, soul, and body, I quiet myself before you now.

As I drift off to sleep, whisper words of revelation and love. Let me hear your sweet soothing voice as you sing over my heart. Bless me with pleasant dreams and dreams that are filled with encounters of your glory. Counsel me with your perfect wisdom and prepare me for what lies ahead.

I thank you that I will fall asleep quickly and have a restful night's sleep. With your angels protecting me, I will fear no evil. Fill my room with the tangible presence of heaven. I will sleep soundly as I rest in your love.

Ascend

My love for your ways is indescribable;
in my innermost being I want to follow them perfectly!
Psalm 119:167

I love you. Those three words seem so insufficient to express what is in my heart. Even if I filled all of the books, in all of the libraries of the world, I wouldn't be able to find the words to describe how much I love you. If I spoke in every language of the world, nonstop, for the rest of my life, I couldn't adequately describe what I feel when I'm with you.

My beautiful Savior and Friend, you have overwhelmed my heart and I will never be the same. I'm bowed before you; the pain I once knew has been washed away by waves of love crashing upon my heart. You have won me over.

The touch of your splendor has kindled a life flowing with grace. You've covered me in light. You've filled the dark spaces with the brilliance of your smile. If only I could find the words to explain what I feel when you are near. The visitations of your glory have left me undone. Since I cannot find the words, I will simply remain here in the stillness of your love.

The Ways of Honor

He turns paupers into princes and seats them
on their royal thrones of honor.

Psalm 113:8

Lord, you are so glorious! You will calm the storms, quell the riots, and deliver the innocent with glory that outshines even the heavens. Above the clamor, I hear you rising from your throne. When wickedness overtakes our land, you will not stay silent.

From sunrise to sunset, you hear the cries of the broken and come to their defense. When you see the poor, you lift them from the dust and teach them the ways of wisdom and prosperity. So many are in despair—wretched and humiliated. Come to their rescue and show them your kindness. Set them on high and teach them the ways of honor.

Even in the most desolate situation, you are there. You restore the destinies of the young and old. No one is out of reach and nothing can separate us from your love. Thank you for your grace and tender mercy. Your faithfulness deserves our greatest praise.

You're the Answer

Display your strength, God, and we'll be strong!
For your miracles have made us who we are.
Psalm 68:28

God, when I look in the mirror, I scarcely recognize who I've become. Countless times you saved me from myself. When I wrestled with you and believed I was stronger without you, you looked on me with mercy and lifted my load. You showed me what true strength was, then placed a royal robe upon me and called me a conqueror. Now, as one of your noble ones, I lead the earth in a procession of worship.

As you kiss me, courage floods my being. So kiss me—kiss the whole world with your redeeming love. Pull the lost out of hiding, so all of the nations of the earth will sing your praise. Pour out your miracles and display your strength. Let the whole world see who you've called them to be. Bless Africa too, Lord! When she sees your majesty, she'll run to you with open arms.

We are consumed with awe as your glory streams from heaven. As you soar upon the clouds of glory, we will sing your highest praise. For you are the answer to our every prayer.

A Life of Grace

I will live enthroned with you forever!
Guard me, God, with your unending, unfailing love.
Let me live my days walking in grace and truth before you.
Psalm 61:7

My life, my very existence is hidden in the paradise of your presence. Wherever I go, the splendor-shadow of your protection covers me. Even when I'm far from home, feeling weak and overwhelmed, you hear me. My cries go straight to your heart and you respond with the compassion and intensity of a father. Your strong hand holds mine and you guide me back into your glory, where I'm safe.

I am your beloved. The strength of your unending and unfailing love overwhelms me. You lavish me with treasures of divine inheritance and treat me like royalty. You've given me a full and abundant life. Oh, that I might walk in grace and truth all of my days and bring honor to your name. I will live and reign with you forever.

I drink from the fountain of your Word—it sustains me. Let my praises fill the heavens as every day I lift my gift of love to you. My resolutions to you remain true. May the glory of your faithfulness flow to my family for generations to come.

Legacy

Shout in celebration of praise to the Lord!
Everyone who loves the Lord and delights in him
will cherish his words and be blessed beyond expectation!
Their descendants will be prosperous and influential.
Every generation of his godly lovers will experience his favor!
Psalm 112:1–2

Lord, your promises have been my delight and I've cherished your words. I've seen your blessing upon my life. I've known your faithfulness—over and over again it has strengthened me. You are committed to me—your covenant will extend beyond my children, through every generation.

Let this be the testimony of my descendants: that they would intimately experience the joys of knowing you. May they walk in the reality of your presence, know the sound of your voice, and receive the comfort of your touch. May they never associate with rebellion, but always follow the way of righteousness.

Even if darkness overtakes them, burst through with your sunrise-brilliance and set them free. Surround them with your favor and fill them with your wisdom. As they conduct themselves with integrity and truth, prosper them and give them influence. May the triumph of faith be their inheritance—a legacy I leave behind.

Steadfast

But now, O Yahweh-God, make yourself real to me
like you promised me you would!
Because of your constant love and your heart-melting kindness,
come be my Hero and deliver me!

Psalm 109:21

Lord, make yourself real to me. I'm worn out, hurt, and broken. The lies people are saying about me have shaken me to the core. I have lived before you with an upright heart. The slandering of my reputation means people won't trust my counsel. They'll miss out on the gifts you've given me to share. Instead of being known as a person of integrity, I'll become the example of failure and shame.

Help me to stay focused. To remain under the covering of your presence while you set things straight. I know you have already won my victory. With the brightness of your truth, uncover each lie that hides in the shadows. For every curse that has been spoken over me, bless me many times more.

Though these people torment me, I'll trust in your constant love and heart-melting kindness. My heart will remain steadfast. I'll pray until I become prayer itself and thank you in advance for all you're about to do.

God of Justice

Then everyone will say, "There is a God who judges the judges";
and "there is a great reward in loving God!"

Psalm 58:11

You are the God of Justice. The One who rules in righteousness and sweeps away oppression. These high and mighty politicians who think that they can get away with bribery and iniquity cannot hide their wicked deeds from you. You see everything and will judge every last one. Your children will celebrate when good triumphs over evil. We will join you in trampling wickedness. Let abuse of power never be known among those who love you.

As for me, I will walk before you in innocence, because I know there is great reward in loving you. You will keep me safe from my enemies. You are the commander of Angel-Armies and you watch over me from your throne. Though evil schemes have been plotted against me, which I've done nothing to deserve, I will trust in you.

Reach down and lift me up, so no evil can touch me. I will not be troubled by the conspiracies of those who misuse their authority. Together we will sit side by side and have a good laugh as we watch their plans fail. It's nice to know that the God of Israel has my back.

To Be One

As for me, because I am innocent I will see your face
until I see you for who you really are.
Then I will awaken with your form and be fully satisfied,
fulfilled in the revelation of your glory in me!

Psalm 17:15

You are the fire that awakens my soul. I see it, blazing through your eyes and igniting my heart. At times I can barely stand in your holy presence, but I'm drawn to the passion behind those eyes. Touch me now. Anoint me, so I may look you fully in the face.

You satisfy my deepest cry: to live ever before your presence. But I want more. I want to see you clearly, with no shadow of sin to blur my vision. Reveal your glory—alive and powerful within me. I am yours.

I worship you. Your love plays a chord within my heart, rousing emotions I didn't know existed. Come closer. Kiss me with unquenchable fire. Burn away the barriers I've erected that would keep you out. Fill me with your righteousness, so we may be one.

Sleeping Hearts

Amazingly, God—so full of compassion—still forgave them.
He covered over their sins with his love,
refusing to destroy them all.
Over and over he held back his anger,
restraining wrath to show them mercy.

Psalm 78:38

How quickly people wander away from you. How soon they forget the epic things you've done for them. My heart grieves for those who disregard your love, only reaching for you when things go bad. You care for them, yet they take it for granted. They limit you by offering worship that has no depth. They talk about you, but don't take the time to get to know you.

Lord, awaken these sleeping hearts. Visit them with the reality of your love. Your mercy is endless—pouring over souls who don't deserve it. Your love is eternal—paid for by redemption's kiss. Remember how frail they are; hold back your anger and come to their rescue.

Don't punish them for their lack of substance. Though their heads are full of knowledge, their hearts are far from you. You are full of compassion—forgive them. Great Shepherd, lead them from the tyranny of doubt and guide them to the border of your holiness. Give them an encounter with your love and they will never be the same.

Where Are You?

*I remembered my worship songs I used to sing
in the night seasons,
and my heart began to fill again with thoughts of you.
So my spirit went out once more in search of you.*

Psalm 77:6

Sometimes I feel as if you're hiding. The silence doesn't beckon and my heart feels dry. I can't seem to find you anywhere. Come out, Lord. I'm searching for you.

I'm shrouded in grave clothes, restricted by the distractions I've entertained. Merciful Savior, pour out your love again. Release me from this season of bewilderment. Find me. Lift me up, because I've fallen in the dust. I'll lie here in wait, singing love songs that flow from my heart.

As soon as I fill my soul with thoughts of you, light begins to shine through the obscurity. Suddenly, I can see again. You were there all along—within reach—if only I would turn my heart to you. Forgive me for being preoccupied with so many other things, when your love is all I need.

Restore My Soul

Lord, you are so good to me, so kind in every way
and ready to forgive,
for your grace-fountain keeps overflowing,
drenching all your lovers who pray to you.

Psalm 86:5

God, you're so good to me. You're gracious and compassionate—the strength of my life. Once again, I desperately need your help. I'm so humbled, Lord. So weak and troubled. I turn to you and no one else. I am your loyal servant, your child, your friend. The one who loves you.

You've never failed me. You're merciful and patient, always coming to my rescue. Even in the midst of tragedy, you have a plan. Lead me back to your fountain of grace and restore my soul. Unveil the deep work of your Spirit in me. Be my Hero once again.

I close my eyes and see you in the midst of pain. Even in the deepest darkness, your extravagant love surrounds me. I lean on you—your steady hand supports me. All I am is yours. Drench me in your love and don't let me go.

Awaken the Earth

Let all your godly-lovers be glad!
Yes, let them all rejoice in your presence
and be carried away with gladness.
Let them laugh and be radiant with joy!

Psalm 68:3

God, I can't help but laugh when I see you riding the clouds and awakening the earth. You sure know how to make an entrance! I knew you would come. Your enemies will scatter in fear, but your godly-lovers will get carried away in celebration. You are our Father, our Friend, our Champion, the God of highest glory and power.

You revive the weary, accompany the lonely, and send reviving rain on parched lands. You lead us through the wilderness and give us joy for mourning. You are our freedom, our Holy God who radiates with contagious bliss! Heartache and despair cannot be found in your presence. You are the momentum that keeps us moving forward.

You fill the skies, shake the earth, and display your power for all to see. Take us to the heights of heaven. Let us soar with you over magnificent mountains. Together we will radiate with beauty—glistening like gold and sparkling like silver through your sacrifice on a wooden cross.

March

Irresistible

*Your extravagant kindness to me
makes me want to follow your words even more!*

Psalm 119:65

Lord, you are irresistible! Your words are entwined within my heart. Your mercy-kiss comforts and restores. Everything you do is beautiful, flowing from your goodness. You are my Friend. The joy I have from walking with you spills over in unrestrained laughter for all the world to hear. Your presence is so powerful and pure.

The power of your words overtakes me and drives me to my knees. How brilliant you are! How amazing! I lift my hands and declare, "You are my true treasure!" All of the riches and wealth in the world cannot compare to the glory of your wisdom.

Your extravagant kindness makes me want to follow you even more. Your hands have held me and made me who I am. I delight in your love. I will boast of your patience and grace. May I be an example of one who loves you wholeheartedly and without restraint, so all your lovers will follow me as I follow you.

The Journey

So I've learned from my experience
that God protects the childlike and humble ones.
For I was broken and brought low,
but he answered me and came to my rescue!

Psalm 116:6

Life with you has taught me many things. Most of all, I've learned how faithful you are. So many times when I was terrified and overcome with sorrow, you dried my tears. Though I asked you for the solution to my problem, you simply held me. You taught me that you alone are the answer to all of my questions and if I have you, I have all that I need.

You are so gracious, so patient. Because of your passion for me, you will always work things out in the end. This is what I must always remember and what I will share with all who listen: No matter how hard things get, even when we feel ourselves slipping into dark shadows, you are there. You never leave us.

For the rest of my days, I have this goal: to relax and rest, confident and serene. Strengthen me so I may fully enjoy my life before you, simply trusting you.

The Wonder of Your Love

Everyone look!
Come and see the breathtaking wonders of our God.

Psalm 46:8

God, when I witness your breathtaking wonders, I stand silent—awestruck by your great power. Though the nations may rage, you simply raise your voice and still the course of madness. Even the mountains move at your command. You are God, Commander, and Mighty Lord of Angel-Armies who will be exalted throughout the earth.

This is why I never need to fear: you are my dwelling place and the shelter in which I hide. Neither raging storm nor blazing fire—nothing will separate me from your love. You are more than capable of keeping me safe, even when the earth quakes and the mountains crash into the sea. Nothing will crush my faith.

With the dawn of daybreak, all will know you are God. And above you, there is none other. We will dive into your rivers of refreshing, which sparkle with joy and delight. We will swim in the waters, which lead to your holy dwelling. There we will gaze upon the One whose might causes both ruin and revival. There we will stand confident in the wonder of your love.

Anointed to Reign

*You have appointed me king and rescued me
time and time again with your magnificent miracles.*

Psalm 18:50

No one keeps their promises like you do, God. You've unlocked the chains that held me captive, empowering me for a life of victory. Guilt and shame fall like lifeless leaves, which cover the ground, only to be trampled underfoot. The way you have transformed me is nothing short of a miracle.

You envelop me with grace, so all who stand before me know I belong to you. In your presence, I'll ascend into the heights of glory with total confidence because I am yours and you are mine. Help me to remember what you've taught me—that my most powerful weapon against the enemy is to worship you. As I do, with all of my attention focused on you, he will fall at my feet in silence and cower in fear. It is your greatness that gives me the victory.

You're merciful and kind. You treat me like a king and anoint me to reign. I honor you for the favor you've given me. Though nations may serve me and obey my every word, I will sing your praises with total abandon and let everyone know I owe it all to you, my Savior and Lord.

Hold Me

Lord, listen to all my tender cries.
Read my every tear, like liquid words
that plead for your help.

Psalm 39:12

I'm no stranger to your love. I know the ways of grace and truth. We have danced upon oppression and sailed through blackened storms of confusion. My hope is anchored in your promises. I know you will make a way. But right now I feel alone. My tears are liquid words, speaking what my voice cannot.

I've set my heart on a pilgrimage—I am yours forever and that will never change. I believe you will part the dark skies, but I've been waiting for so long. I'm tired. Today, all I can do is cry. Come. Hold me.

I will find the joy beyond this suffering. You will kiss me with restoration. Once again I will walk upon the breath of grace. But not right now. Right now I am enfolded in your arms and this is where I'll stay.

You will hold me until the pain stops; until I am quiet and can hear you speak.

Restoration

Let my passion for life be restored,
tasting joy in every breakthrough you bring to me.
Give me more of your Holy Spirit-Wind
so that I may stand strong and true to you!

Psalm 51:12

Lord, I want to taste joy that is pure and bright. The joy that flows from the fountain of your great pleasure. I bow low, asking you to blow the winds of your Spirit upon me and restore me fully. Then I will know the love that unlocks my heart, so my lips will flow with songs of uncontainable praise. Break through for me and help me to stand strong, so I never lose my way again.

You're loving and merciful, never despising a shattered heart. All can find their way back to you when overtaken by the weaknesses of their flesh. I know this for a fact, because you've restored my soul and delivered me from evil. You didn't punish me; instead you brought me close to you, wrapped me in your love, and restored my passion. It's your kindness that leads me to repentance. In you I've found my home—my source of joy.

Merciful King

The heavens respond:
"God himself will be their Judge,
And he will judge them with righteousness!"
Psalm 50:6

God, you present yourself to us in every brilliant sunrise and each painted sunset. With each crack of lightning, we witness the blazing brilliance of your being. Your steps are heard in each rumble of thunder. Your crown blazes with fiery glory, illuminating the earth. You are the mighty God, the God of Power, the Great I Am.

Radiant in perfected beauty, you come to your courtroom to judge in righteousness. You are not like us—you are holy, undefiled, the only trustworthy and honorable one who will set things right. The heavens declare your justice.

The entire world and everything it contains is yours, yet you take time for me. You faithfully delight in my sacrifices of praise, which I lay at your feet. Merciful King, I offer you my heart, which has never strayed, and my words that seek only to honor you. Unfold your continuing salvation to me; I kneel before you now and trust you to judge me rightly.

Quicksand

Arise, awake, and come to help us, O Lord.
Let your unfailing love save us from this sorrow!
Psalm 44:26

Lord, I'm facedown before you. It feels as if I'm sinking in quicksand, abandoned by you in this wilderness—this dark night of the soul. You know every secret of my heart and you know I'm forever yours. I haven't broken covenant with you, nor will I. Though you are silent, I will worship you.

I will remind myself of the miracles I read about, of battles won, not by the strength of mortals, but through the displays of your mighty power. Your radiant-presence shined forth and delivered many before me. Victory was theirs because you loved them. Victory will be mine because you love me.

Your love is endless and unfailing. This is what I must always remember: even when I can't feel it, your love is ever present. The miracles you've done for others, you want to do for me. I'll shake off this discouragement and trust in you again. You are my Savior! You'll never let me down!

You Still Love Me

*Lord, don't hold back your love or withhold
your tender mercies from me.
Keep me in your truth and let your compassion overflow to me
no matter what I face.*

Psalm 40:11

No one knows me the way you do, Lord. So I won't pretend I'm something that I'm not. I know your Word and I've taught others about your faithfulness. I try so hard not to grumble or speak out of my disappointment, because I know the truth. I have no excuse. In the most painful moments, when it feels as if you aren't answering me, my heart burns and thoughts spew from my lips.

When I focus on my sin, guilt pushes my head to the ground with a heavy hand, and I'm ashamed to look at you. But then I remember your tender mercy. The way you always restore me and see me through the eyes of love. The truth is, without you I won't make it through this life. I'll always need you. Always need a Savior.

I guess that's what makes me love you more—knowing how frail I am and that graciously, you still love me.

Extravagant Mercy

But you, O Lord, your mercy-seat love is limitless,
reaching higher than the highest heavens.

Psalm 36:5

Your mercy is astounding! I can't help but laugh when I see the wicked fighting against you like ants trying to take on a mountain. If only they could see how silly they look trying to take on the holy God. When I turn to you, to see what you'll do, you astound me. You judge with wisdom and righteousness, yet your extravagant mercy reaches to everyone; it leaves no one out.

You stretch out your wings for all of humankind to take refuge. Your mercy makes no exclusions, once a heart is turned to you. Your love is a flowing fountain of delight for all who will partake. These are the springs of life that quench the thirsty soul.

Smear the anointing of your love upon our hearts, so all may truly know you. Release your blessing upon the lives of those who choose you. We will run through heaven's halls, shouting your praise! Your holiness draws us like a moth to the light. Nothing satisfies like your extravagant love. Nothing compares to your extravagant mercy.

Holy Pursuit

Lord, who dares to dwell with you?
Who presumes the privilege of being close to you,
living next to you in your shining place of glory?
Who are those who daily dwell in the life of the Holy Spirit?

Psalm 15:1

It's true. I'm one of the ones who dare to believe I can dwell with you. Your glory shines brightly, but it isn't presumption that makes me bold. I endeavor to stand within your brilliant radiance only because I have come in humility; my only aim: to honor you with my life.

May I always be passionate and sincere, trustworthy and honest. May my ears never delight in slander; may my words always be honorable. Lord, you applaud those who follow truth, who are faithful, and who seek you with wholehearted passion. This is who I desire to be.

I commit myself to living daily in your holy presence. You have honored me with your nearness and I flourish in your grace. Your love is like a holy fire, burning away all desire for frivolous pursuits. Your majesty brings me to my knees. I bow before you, my Lord and my King, humbly submitting every part of me. To worship you, my greatest delight.

Bless the Children

Children are God's love-gift; they are heaven's generous reward. ...
Happy will be the couple who has many of them!
A household full of children will not bring shame on your name
but victory when you face your enemies,
for your kids will have influence and honor
to prevail on your behalf!
Psalm 127:3, 5

Father, bless the children. Make yourself irresistibly real to each one. Draw them close to you and protect them, spirit, soul, and body. Plant your words deep within their hearts, so they will never depart. May they grow in grace and wisdom, all the days of their lives.

Let sounds of joy replace tattered hearts that need your love and intervention. Surround each child with your holy angels who will guard them from harm. Remove those who are in unsafe situations and put them in places of refuge and peace. Give each child a home where they are loved and cared for.

May they learn to climb every mountain that stands in their way and become courageous followers of your truth. Let their love for you be uncompromising and teach them to love others without restriction. Let this generation, and the many who will follow, know their true identity in you and be confident. Cause them to run with purity, integrity, holiness, kindness, and compassion into this world, so they fill it to overflowing.

My Only Hope

God, I'm crying out to you!
I lift up my voice boldly to beg for your mercy!
I spill out my heart to you and tell you all my troubles.

Psalm 142:1–2

Lord, I feel stuck. Nothing is working out the way I thought it would. Life has become a whirlwind of opposition and I have no one to turn to but you. You're my only hope and my sole means of escape. Come and turn my mourning into dancing once again.

At times I feel like King David, alone and hiding in a cave. But these limitations go deeper than my surroundings and into the depth of my soul. My mind has been hijacked by constant anxiety and worry. You seem so far away.

I lift my voice with cries for mercy and wonder if you hear or if you're moved by my tears. As I sit in silence, the breath of your Spirit falls upon my ears and I hear one word: *believe*. This is what moves your heart—my faith.

Forgive me for doubting, for magnifying problems when I should be glorifying you. I will remember this truth: Every provision has already been made. All I need to do is fall back into the grace that has always been there and rest in your love. You will take care of the rest.

Provider

The Lord is my Fierce Protector and my Pastor.
I always have more than enough.

Psalm 23:1

God, you are my Provider. Everything I need comes from you, my source of endless blessing. As I seek you first, you will shower me with more than I need; you will give me the desires of my heart.

You love me and have nothing but the best in store for me. Your plans are designed to prosper me and give me a future filled with hope. Lack is a curse I will not accept. Give me wisdom and power to create wealth, so I will have more than enough to be a blessing to others. Teach me things I haven't known before. Open doors of favor that launch me into divine opportunities. Bless the work of my hands.

You have designed me to live a glorious life free from stress and worry. You want me to prosper and be in health, even as my soul prospers. So, I will not worry about tomorrow. I will trust you to be my Shepherd and lead me forth. You've given me a beautiful inheritance.

Forgive

Righteousness is revealed every time you judge.
Because of the strength of your forgiveness,
your anger does not break out every day
even though you are a righteous Judge.

Psalm 7:11

Your forgiveness knows no bounds. It is not limited, even by your righteous anger. Help me to be like you. Give me grace as I learn to forgive; heal me of memories that trigger painful emotions.

I will not be held prisoner by bitterness and offense. No matter what anyone has done to me, and regardless of how unfair or terrible it was, I refuse to live in torment. I make the decision today to live in the freedom purchased for me on the cross. Anytime I see those who hurt me, I hear their names, or a thought pops up about them, I will arrest that thought and give it to you. I will release forgiveness to them, even if I have to do it many times each day.

I lay aside my right to be angry or hurt. Instead of feeling empowered by holding on to anger, I will enjoy the power of hope and joy. Give me peace in place of anger and pain. Help me see through your eyes those who've hurt me. Cause me to be victorious and free by choosing to forgive.

Flood

My enemies have chased and caught me
and crushed my life into dust. ...
Now I'm reaching out to you, thirsting for you
like the dry, cracked ground thirsts for rain.

Psalm 143:3, 6

Lord, I thirst for your living waters. Flood my soul and saturate every fiber of my being with waves of refreshing. I'm not satisfied with the touch of yesterday's encounters. Every day I must have more of you. Your presence is tangible when I step beyond the veil.

My heart is in a continual state of longing. I'm reaching for you—the only thing that satisfies. I live in a perpetual mystery—being filled, yet wanting more. Your love is never-ending. Discovering you is unlike any other joy I've known. You are so good to me.

Let the wells of glory within my spirit rise until they overflow. I want to drip with your holy love everywhere I go. When people look at me, I want them to see you looking back. I want them to see the smile that has changed my life, so it will transform theirs as well.

Meet with me. There is nothing I want more.

Let Go

I come before your presence with my sacrifice.
I'll give you all that I've promised, everything I have.

Psalm 66:13

God, I'm yours. I hold nothing back. My heart, my soul, and strength—I give to you what you first gave to me. I hold in my hands every thought I have and offer to you what you've already known was there. All that I am and hope to be, every dream and goal, each failure and fear, I surrender to your grace.

You knew me before you formed me in my mother's womb. There is nothing hidden from the One who sees it all. As I look back over the years, I see the imprints of your love that have sealed my heart. You drew me by your grace and held me close, though I did nothing to deserve it.

At times I hid from the reflection of myself that I saw in your eyes, yet you never stopped believing in me. Now everything I am is yours. I let go of it all and reach for your hand. I'm excited to see where your love will take me.

My Fortress

There is only one strong, safe, and secure place for me;
it's in God alone and I love him!
He's the One who gives me strength and skill for the battle.

Psalm 144:1

God, my eyes are firmly fixed upon you. Though the enemy stands before me like a giant, I will trust in you, for you are my Shelter of love and my Fortress of faith. You are the One who strengthens me and delivers me from the powers of darkness. Step down from heaven, Lord, and overthrow the evil looming over me.

Your love is faithful and true. My life is nothing more than a faint whisper or a mere breath, yet you delight in me. You will reach down from heaven and rescue me. You are my Mighty Deliverer who fights for me with one hand and tenderly embraces me with the other.

Together we will see the enemy run in terror! Songs of love flow effortlessly from my lips as I anticipate the victory. The harp inside my heart praises you with beautiful melody.

How Can It Be?

I said to the Lord God,
"You are my Maker, my Mediator, and my Master.
Any good thing you find in me has come from you."
And he said to me, "My holy lovers are wonderful,
my majestic ones, my glorious ones,
fulfilling all my desires."

Psalm 16:2–3

I run to you, God. There is no other place I'd rather be than safe in your arms. No one knows me the way you do. You're my Maker, Mediator, and Master. There is nothing I could possibly offer you that hasn't come from your hands. You certainly aren't impressed with my goodness. I am nothing apart from you.

Yet as I look into your face, you declare something more remarkable and glorious than anything I've heard before. You say I'm majestic, wonderful, and glorious. In ways I cannot understand, I fulfill you. Those words stir me more deeply than any words ever spoken. It is unfathomable that you, the mighty God, could think this way about me.

Declarations of your incomprehensible love inspire me to be all you've created me to be. You've engraved your very nature into my heart with a seal of golden glory. I will never escape your unrelenting love, nor do I want to.

God's Unashamed Love

The Lord looks down in love,
bending over heaven's balcony,
looking over all of Adam's sons and daughters.
He's looking to see if there is anyone who acts wisely,
any who are searching for God and wanting to please him.

Psalm 14:2

Lord, I feel sorry for those who think there is no God. Who stumble and fall, but refuse to pray—afraid they just might discover you for themselves. I don't understand why anyone would want to resist a love like yours. A love so radiant and fascinating, it's beyond compare.

With great compassion you bend over the balcony of heaven, searching the earth for those whose hearts are toward you. What a beautiful sight, to see you, the God of Zion, leaning in close, unashamed of your love for humankind. Let me love you this way—devotion that is free from pride, a heart humble enough to show the world.

May our generation be known as loyal lovers. We search for you in every situation. We carry ourselves with wisdom and compassion. You have restored us to yourself. You call us your very own. We look to you with indescribable joy, expecting to see you face-to-face.

Astounding

O God, to the farthest corners of the planet
people will stand in awe,
startled and stunned by your signs and wonders.

Psalm 65:8

When I consider your power—your ability to breathe substance into each desire of your heart and then share it with us through creation—my mouth hangs wide open. You are the confidence of the entire planet! There is no escaping your beautiful creation. I see your handiwork in every nation of the world, even to the farthest islands.

Sometimes I like to sit back and bask in the wonder of your artistry, on display before me. How astounding it is! Majestic mountains set in place by your hand, the vast expanse of roaring seas echoing your voice, the sunrise and sunset both casting tranquility upon the land. May I never take your brilliance for granted, and always remember you are speaking, even in the softest breeze.

Your visitations of glory saturate the earth with blessing, infusing us with peace. Even the wheels of your chariot drip with oil. You quell the rages of the angriest mobs, you explode the misconceptions of human bigotry, and under the same star-lit sky, you remind us you are the righteous God who loves us all.

Redeeming Love

I will give my thanks to you from a heart of love and truth.
And every time I learn more of your righteous judgments,
I will be faithful to all that your Word reveals—
so don't ever give up on me!

Psalm 119:7–8

Lord, you never give up on me. Even when I tried to go my own way and do my own thing, you never left my side. Though I clothed myself in shadows, trying to find a place to hide, you saw me. You found the tiniest crevice where you could reach me, then you poured in the light of your love to draw me out. You were my defining moment.

Now I know that I will only know true happiness when I walk in total integrity. You are my heart's passion and when I seek you, joy overwhelms me. You have prescribed the right way for me to live. To ignore it is foolish. To follow it is joy unspeakable. I thought I knew how to find success, but without peace, I attained nothing.

You are my strength. I will choose you forever. Thank you for your redeeming love.

Life's Greatest Quest

Lord, you are great and worthy of the highest praise!
For there is no end to the discovery
of the greatness that surrounds you.

Psalm 145:3

It will take all of eternity to fully discover the greatness of your glory. Even now, as I kneel before you, I'm undone by these limited encounters—trinkets of splendor that are nothing compared to the glory yet to be revealed. Flood my being with treasures of your love.

I wonder how much more of your presence I can take. What limit is there to the amount of glory my body can handle? I don't know, but I want to find out. Lord, unveil your magnificent splendor until there is nothing left in me that doesn't reflect you. I want you, filling every part of me.

You are my great obsession. Day and night I meditate on your love and search the Scriptures for truth. One touch of your presence leaves me trembling—satisfied yet overcome with yearning. I'm left with no other choice than to live here, in this place of relentless pursuit. You are everything I hold dear, life's greatest quest.

A Worshiping Creation

Let the earth join in with this parade of praise!
You mighty creatures of the ocean's depths,
echo in exaltation!

Psalm 148:7

Praise arises from the brilliance of your creation. The stars dance to the music of a cosmic symphony, flowers bow beneath celebrations of wind, while oceans rejoice with the sound of crashing cymbals. Even the beasts of the fields lift their voices with roars of celebration. Yes, the work of your hands lives to honor you.

Alongside these, I will sing. For nothing brings you more delight than hearing your children rejoice. Clothed in the radiant beauty of a surrendered heart, I offer you my sincere devotion and fervent praise. For you are my Father, my Savior, and my Best Friend.

Ever faithfully, you guide me on my journey. You protect me and counsel me with perfected wisdom. When I see your glory, I can't help but smile. I am created in your image—I look like you! Though nature praises you as Creator, only I can offer you the love of a cherished child.

Reveal

Beloved ones, listen to this instruction.
Open your heart to the revelation
of this mystery that I share with you.
Psalm 78:1

Lord, make me a voice of truth, sharing masterfully about all you've done. Let my words reveal the mystery of the ages—the answers found only in you. Help me to pass down more than fables by instilling enduring faith to all who hear. Let me express more than an intriguing riddle.

May every person who listens open their hearts to understand the rich heritage we have in you. For generations to come, may my children remember your faithfulness and follow your ways. Let them truly love you with hearts that never stray, even when they grow old.

Breathe upon every mention I make of you. Let my speech be alive, like a cloud of glory or a pillar of fire that leads the way. In times of dryness, let these words flow like a river, quenching the deepest thirst. May we never dishonor you with simple words that have no substance. Let our abundant hearts swell and overflow with evidence of your love.

Vibrant

Pour into me the brightness of your daybreak!
Pour into me your rays of revelation-truth!
Let them comfort and gently lead me onto the shining path,
showing the way into your burning presence,
into your many sanctuaries of holiness.

Psalm 43:3

Father, I want to come closer to you—to your very altar. Show me the way into your burning presence. Illuminate my path with truth and lead the way into your many sanctuaries of holiness. I'll run through your halls with a roaring heart of passion, seeking those eyes ablaze with fire.

Magnificent God, you are my Protector, the One who pleads my case and destroys my walls of insecurity and fear. No one can steal my peace—I won't let them. With you at my side, I won't be afraid of what the future holds, no matter how obscure it may look to me at the moment.

Laying all of my fears at your feet and choosing to trust in your promises gives me the fortitude to carry on. Bowing low before your presence, I see rays of glory pool around me. Suddenly I'm filled with uncontainable joy. It bursts forth with cries of praise that will never stop! Vibrant and alive—that's what life with you is like.

Close to Me

I will sing my song of joy to you, the Most High,
for in all of this you have strengthened my soul.
My enemies say that I have no Savior,
but I know that I have one in you!

Psalm 13:6

My soul is shaken and it feels as though the enemy is prevailing. Lord, I'm not sure how much more I can take. Turn your eyes in my direction, and answer me as you've always done. Your kindness has never failed me before.

Darkness has tried to blind me from the hope I have in you. But then you illuminate my soul with one glimpse of your glorious light and I can see again. I can feel again—you're breathing life into my spirit, reminding me of your nearness. You're close to me, so very close, as you've always been.

How faithfully you take the most difficult of times and use them to strengthen my soul. I will not despise the lessons you teach me along the way. You are my Savior who turns everything around for my good. You are my song of joy and with a thankful heart I will celebrate this love, unmatched by any other.

Because You Love Me

The intense pleasure you give me
surpasses the gladness of harvest time,
even more than when the harvesters
gaze upon their ripened grain
and when their new wine overflows.

Psalm 4:7

When trouble rears its head, squeezing the life out of me, I remind myself you are my Champion. At times my faith is nothing more than a weak sacrifice, yet in ways unknown to me, it pleases you. Not only do you hear every prayer I pray, you answer me with kindness and work wonders for me, all because you love me. What an inspiration you are!

I ponder your love and peace fills my being. There you are—I can feel the warmth of your radiant face. Light spills through the darkness and pools around me in waves of glory. Your presence stills my heart. Suddenly, I can breathe again.

Now I know—truly know—that no matter what, you will break through for me. Your love is liberating; it frees me and fills me with joy greater than I've ever known. I'm like someone intoxicated with wine, free as a bird with not a care in the world. Oh, how I love you, Lord! Your kindness fills me with laughter!

Longings

I am continually consumed by these irresistible longings,
these cravings to obey your every commandment!
Psalm 119:20

I am continually consumed by irresistible longings to follow you. As I walk humbly in your truth, I will see with your eyes and hear by your Spirit. I want to be like you—sympathizing with the inclinations of mortals. Fill me with your understanding and tutor me in your ways. May my heart and mind flow in unison with your Holy Spirit.

Open my understanding to see the miracle-wonders hidden in your Word. Your wisdom both supports and contradicts the brilliance of mortals, encouraging me to dive deeper into your depths. Your revelation-light is eternal. It speaks from eternity past to eternity forward.

Connect me to your heart as I ponder your words. Let the desires that drive my life be pleasing in your sight. I seek your favor. I long for the reality of your touch. You are the joyful meditation of my soul.

Holy Place

Lord, aren't we your beloved dove that praises you?
Protect us from these wild beasts who want to harm us.
Don't leave us as lambs among wolves!
You can't abandon us after all we've been through!

Psalm 74:19

I will always need you. Whether in the midst of devastation or in the beauty of triumph, you are my everything. When situations hold me back and I don't know how to proceed, you part the seas and make a way. When the enemy comes to wreak havoc in my life, I know that his only goal is to separate me from you. I will cherish the sanctity of my union with you and defeat him from the place of rest. Loving and trusting you is the greatest form of warfare.

You are my King and my Mighty Conqueror. Your promises strengthen me. I will not fear, as if a lamb among wolves. When I worship, unleash your might. Let your glory reveal evil lurking in the shadows, so the wicked have no place to hide. I stand confident in your keeping power. I am your beloved dove, perfected by your beauty.

You own the day and bless the night. Your wonders are seen throughout the earth. You paint the seasons and calm the storms. My hope is in you. My heart is your holy place.

Weary

Lord, you know my prayer before I even whisper it.
At each and every sunrise you will
continue to hear my cry until you answer.

Psalm 88:13

God, you know everything I need, even before I ask. But I've asked—many times over. Though my prayers have turned to whispers, I will not quit. Every morning I will come before your throne and wait for your answer.

Waves of glory that crashed upon my soul have turned to clouds of dust. Send your healing rain and wash me in your love once again. Life is colorless and dreary when I lose sight of you. My arms, though weak, are stretched out to you, my only Redeemer.

Fan the flame within my heart. I'm desperate for you. Needing more than answers, I seek the light of your face. Though delay has made me weary, you will make me strong. Your strength is perfected in my weakness. Covenant-keeping God, I know that what you've promised, you will do.

April

What Love Can Do

Your anointing has made me strong and mighty.
You've empowered my life for triumph
by pouring fresh oil over me!

Psalm 92:10

I'm stronger than I thought. I can climb mountains I didn't think I could climb, all because of you. You take me by the hand and together we leap over fences that try to keep us out. Nothing will stop me from fulfilling my destiny. No one will ever convince me your love is not enough.

The cross has triumphed over the enemy. You are the earth's great Champion. You are my Hero and you taught me how to fight. You taught me the power of a willing heart and an obedient soul. You've shown me what love can do.

The fire in your eyes is felt deep within my veins. It kindles a faith I've never known before. The oil of your Spirit heals every wound, reviving my hope and making me bold. There's nothing I can't do when I'm alive in you.

Today

When I had nothing—desperate and defeated,
I cried out to the Lord and he heard me,
bringing his miracle-deliverance when I needed it most.
The angels stooped down to listen as I prayed,
encircling me, empowering me, and showing me how to escape.
They will do this for everyone who fears God.

Psalm 34:6–7

Today is my day of deliverance. No longer will I be defeated by fear, discouragement, sickness, or lack. I will see your promises manifest in my life. It is time for restoration!

God, you said that if I decree your truth and believe it in my heart, it would be established on the earth. So today I declare that the same Spirit that rose Jesus from the dead, abides powerfully inside of me. Whatever I pray in faith, in connection to your promises, you bring to pass. Every shackle that has held me down is broken. I experience peace, joy, wisdom, health, and favor as I walk with you. Every time I call out to you, you manifest the power of your presence in my life.

You have given me authority and power over all of the powers of darkness. Everything the enemy has stolen is being returned to me sevenfold. From this point on, I declare that my life lines up with heaven. I am not a victim. I am victorious in every area of my life because you love me!

Divine Helper

But the Lord God has become my divine Helper!
He leans into my heart and lays his hands upon me!

Psalm 54:4

God, surround me with yourself. For your name's sake, defend me and rescue me from every trouble. When you lean over the balcony of heaven, to see if any have turned their heart to you, lean even closer—into my heart—and see that I am fully yours. See me through the eyes of love. I offer myself freely and unreservedly to you.

The foolish soul thinks they don't need you. They are withering and lost as they wander through life with calloused hearts. Though they have risen against me, I will trust in your great faithfulness. You will lay your hands upon me and sustain me. You are my divine Helper, a wall of protection around me. Through you I will thrive in all I do. I will triumph in the midst of adversity and praise your name, because it is precious to me. Everything I am is yours.

Escaping the Wilderness

I say to myself, "If only I could fly away from all of this!
If only I could run away to the place of rest and peace.
I would run far away where no one could find me,
escaping to a wilderness retreat."

Psalm 55:6–7

Lord, don't let my heart grow dim. Don't let these difficult circumstances steal the affection I have for you, by overwhelming my mind. All I want to do is get as far away from the stress as I can and shake off the heaviness. If only I could hide myself on a tropical paradise and leave it all behind.

But I know that's not the answer. The truth is that you are the peace that surpasses all understanding. You are my paradise. I don't need to run anywhere other than your presence. Regardless of how hard it can get, I must choose the path that leads to you.

Infuse me with grace, so I can stand in the midst of this storm. As I lean into you, clear away the cobwebs of confusion that plague my thoughts. Touch my eyes, so I can see things from your perspective. Breathe fresh resolve into my faith. I know everything I need to get through this comes from you. You came out of the wilderness in power and so will I!

The Beauty of Wisdom

I can never forget the profound revelations you've taught me,
for they have kept me alive more than once.

Psalm 119:93

What a beautiful treasure of understanding unfolds when you instruct me. My entire being is set on fire when you unravel your mysteries within my heart. I long for your truth. I crave the understanding only you can feed me.

You created the entire universe, and everything in it, out of nothing. You are the very substance of wisdom. Your knowledge is limitless. God of wonders, wind, and fire, I honor your perfected brilliance. The most revered genius on earth has barely discovered a fraction of all you know.

Lord, thank you for the many times your wisdom has guided me. Without it, I don't know where I'd be. Open your Word to me continually, so it will have supremacy in my life. I want to climb the highest peaks of understanding, while remaining humble and true. Pierce my heart with fresh revelation and I will come alive.

Government

*O God, make the king a godly judge like you
and give the king's son the gift of justice too.*

Psalm 72:1

God, bless our government. Give our leaders godly insight to judge rightly and mirror your integrity. Bless them. Fill them with divine wisdom, so they will walk honorably and give justice to all. There is none as righteous as you, and our leaders need your guidance.

We cry out for you to rule from sea to sea, as distant kings from every continent and coastland yield their lives to you. For truly, you hold all hearts, great and small, in your hands. You are the King of all kings and through your reign, peace will govern the lands and every nation will bow before your throne.

Let the earth overflow with your glory, your children douse their communities with love, and every mountain of influence blossom with exemplary fruit. May both rich and poor find audience with their King, for your compassion saves our souls. Shower the earth with your rains of revival. Our devotion to you, our inextinguishable love will outlast the sun. For you are the earth's true King.

Living under an Open Heaven

Hallelujah! Praise the Lord! Let the skies be filled with praise and the highest heavens with the shouts of glory!

Psalm 148:1

Father, I praise you for the atmosphere of glory I live in. I will shout with joy, for your Spirit lives inside of me and the heavens are open over my life. Everywhere I go becomes a zone of awakening, turning hearts to you.

God, you are all-powerful and you inhabit my praise. You have lightning in your hands. Together we shift environments. My praise will shake the heavens and set the prisoners free. In any area where my family or I are prisoners to debt, strife, anxiety, or fear, I declare by faith that we have been set free.

Bless me with peace, joy, abundance, and angelic visitations as your glory streams into my life. Let there be constant, unobstructed communion with you in ways that surprise me. Teach me to access answers from heaven and pull them to earth. My prayers go straight to your throne. You hear every word I say. Your favor surrounds me and my cup overflows.

Right Here

It's here in your presence, in your sanctuary,
where I learn more of your ways.
For holiness is revealed in everything you do!
Lord, you're the One and Only, the great and glorious God!

Psalm 77:13

This is where I need to stay—right here in your presence, where you open my eyes to truth and teach me your ways. You are glorious and everything you do is good, but sometimes I forget. Sometimes I let myself get distracted by these trials. When I look away from you and give into the fear, everything goes haywire—I can't even think straight. I find myself yelling for you, as if you have disappeared. How quickly I yield to the pressure.

Then, just as suddenly as I lost my peace, flickers of truth illuminate my mind. I remember how faithful you've been. And when I begin to ponder these things, you burst in with awesome displays of power. The sky explodes with lightning as you make your presence known. Thunder rumbles through the sky, announcing your side of the story, loud and clear.

How foolish I am to ever doubt your love and faithfulness. Even when I cannot see which way to go, your footprints create a path for me to follow. Yes, here is where I need to stay—in your presence, the place of peace.

Fresh Start

*Please, God, don't hold the sins of our fathers against us.
Don't make us pay for their sins.
Hurry to our side, and let your tenderhearted mercy
meet us in our need, for we are devastated beyond belief.*

Psalm 79:8

God, don't let me suffer for the sins of my ancestors. I know their actions set a course for generations to come. Though I choose to follow you, my destiny seems threatened because of their influence upon my life. I can't seem to get a break. Sometimes people scoff, thinking I must be just like them, but they don't know me the way you do.

These are the lies I've been plagued with, but the truth is, you will avenge me and give me a fresh start. I've suffered enough! I will not pay the price for their foolishness. You are my inheritance. Your anger over their sins has been satisfied through the sacrifice of your love. Though I've been devastated and looked down upon, you will come through for me.

Renew my mind and teach me your ways. God of Breakthrough, meet me with your tenderhearted mercy. Hurry to my side and be my Hero. Set my life on a new course as I walk the path you've set for me. Now I will start a new tradition—one of holiness and integrity—praising your name from generation to generation. This is the power of your love.

Fruitful

*Revive us, O God! Let your beaming face shine upon us
with the sunrise rays of glory;
then nothing will be able to stop us.*

Psalm 80:3

Restore, refresh, and revive me, God. I'm worn out and I need your touch. I can't seem to fix things, but you can. This time of darkness seeks to extinguish my faith, but I won't let it. Instead, I will lift my head and allow each crisis to push me closer to you. For you are the only answer.

Listen to my heart's cry and reveal yourself in splendor. Drown my persistent sorrows in your affection. You've always led me so perfectly—I know you won't abandon me now. Shine your radiant countenance upon me. Ride upon the cherubim and come rushing to my side.

For you have called me your fragrant garden, a vineyard that yields a most fruitful harvest. Though you ask me to feed the nations, the fences of protection are broken down and the enemy is stealing the fruit from my vines.

Unless you come and care for me, your garden, I'll be stripped bare—my life will have nothing to show for it. Shine your beaming face upon me and I'll flourish once again. In the glory of your delight, I'll be doubly fruitful. In you, I'll find my way.

Forgiven

*Lord, your love has poured out
so many amazing blessings on our land!
You've restored Israel's destiny from captivity.
You've forgiven our many sins and covered
every one of them in your love.*

Psalm 85:1–2

I stand in silence, waiting for your hand of judgment, but it doesn't come. Instead, against the backdrop of falling rain, I hear you whisper one word: *forgiven*. Though your blazing wrath should be kindled against me, it is extinguished by your mercy—cleansed by drops of holy blood. It is the message of peace I have longed to hear. I can breathe again.

Out of death, life has come. Pour out your Spirit upon me and revive me fully. Shine your power and presence upon my life with the promise of peace. Your sacrifice of love has given me a fresh start. I feel your kiss upon my life.

Your blessings pour down one after the other. Flowers of your faithfulness bloom upon the earth. Mercy and truth have been married. I humbly bow before you and ask for grace, so I will never turn back. I've tasted joy and gladness—the way of life with you.

A Pleasing Offering

Lord, I'm all yours, and you are my Savior;
I have sought to live my life pleasing to you.
Psalm 119:94

God, I was created for you and you alone. All I am and think and do is for your glory. Purify me and set me apart. Transform me into your likeness. I abandon myself to your goodness and offer you my heart.

Your love has saved me. Because of your great mercy, I am free. I am no longer a slave to sin or fear. I am yours—totally and completely surrendered to your will. Nothing else matters to me, other than living in this place of full abandon.

Shine the spotlight of your searching gaze upon my soul and create in me a clean heart. May the soil of my life be good ground, so the seeds of your Word will grow and blossom. I want to be so fully immersed in your dazzling light that I become transparent—a vessel of your presence that draws others to you. I want nothing more than to please you, my beautiful Savior.

The Spirit of the Lord

I am your only God, the Living God!
Wasn't I the One who broke the strongholds over you
and raised you up out of bondage?

Psalm 81:10

Lord, let your Spirit rest upon me. Flood me with yourself. I want to live in perfect unity with you. When people come near me, I want them to feel your tangible presence.

Manifest your presence in and through me, so it radiates from me everywhere I go. Let me hear your voice clearly as I step out to prophesy words of encouragement to others. When I pray for them, let them feel your tangible touch. May your love and wisdom drip from my lips as I speak, so those who listen will hear your voice. Pierce their hearts, so that long after I'm done, my words will linger deep within.

Your presence is alive. Anoint me with your Spirit and I will become another person, doing things I've never done before. Breathe into me, so that when I exhale, it becomes revelation to others. Holy Spirit, be my Best Friend. Teach me all things. You are the door to truth. Release the Spirit of the Lord upon my life.

The Spirit of Wisdom

*For wisdom will come from my mouth,
words of insight and understanding will be heard
from the musings of my heart.*

Psalm 49:3

Father, you promised to fill me with wisdom if I cried out for it and searched for it as for a buried treasure. So that's what I'm doing. I need the Spirit of Wisdom to guide me in every decision I make. Show me which way to go, whether the choices I'm facing are big or small. I want to step with confidence in the direction you're leading and not rely on my own limited understanding. Fill my heart with insight. Give me clarity.

Anoint every word I say, so others will be blessed and encouraged. When I open my mouth, let wisdom pour forth with kindness. May it bring grace to all who hear.

When circumstances are bleak, let wisdom and creativity work together to create surprising opportunities. May I never be discouraged by insurmountable tasks, but with faith, I will trust in your ability to direct me. Your wisdom will cause me to prosper in every situation.

The Spirit of Understanding

*Open up my understanding to the ways of your wisdom
and I will meditate deeply on your splendor and your wonders.*

Psalm 119:27

God, I desire the fullness of who you are to abide powerfully within me. I won't pick and choose which truths to believe—I believe them all! Give me the Spirit of Understanding, so I will know how to apply the wisdom you give me. Place this mantle upon me, the one Jesus had when he walked this earth.

When I walk with true understanding, I will have insight to shift the situations around me. I will know how to implement creative ideas and business plans. You will anoint me to easily solve any problem I face. Solutions will rise from deep within me, bringing the answers that I need.

I'm crying out for understanding that goes far beyond what I perceive with my natural intelligence. Give me discernment that helps me to understand the hearts of others. I will know exactly what to do to set others free.

Today, by faith, I receive the Spirit of Understanding.

The Spirit of Counsel

I speak continually of your laws
as I recite out loud your counsel to me.
Psalm 119:13

Lord, with passionate devotion I pursue you. I want every aspect of your divine nature to saturate my life and flow through me. Fill me with the Spirit of Counsel.

When you counsel me, I know you will lead me in the right direction. You will steer me and guide me in all of my decisions. Pour out the perfection of your thoughts into my heart, so I know which way to go.

When the Spirit of Counsel is upon my life, I will be at the right place at the right time. Divine encounters with those you want to connect me with will be common. As long as I'm walking with you, I will not veer away from my destiny. I will always make wise choices.

You are the wonderful Counselor. Every day I will lean in to hear what you have to say. Anoint my words with your life-giving counsel, so I will release it to others. With wisdom, counsel, and guidance to make good decisions, I can never go wrong.

The Spirit of Power

With you as my strength I can crush an enemy horde
advancing through every stronghold that stands in front of me.

Psalm 18:29

God, I will not relent until I am all you created me to be. Today I rise up in tenacious faith and ask that you would bless me with the Spirit of Power. Give me the same Spirit that empowered David to defeat Goliath with a sling and a stone.

I will not miss my day of visitation. I will tap into your limitless power and see miracles, signs, and wonders flow through my hands. Heaven will be released upon the earth as I reach out with bold faith. I will not back off until I have it all.

Anoint me with boldness and courage when I face the enemy. I will not sit by and allow him to steal, kill, and destroy. The hierarchies of darkness are dismantled when the Spirit of Power comes upon me. Your Spirit within me is greater than any foe—no enemy stands a chance. You haven't given me a spirit of fear! I wear your armor and look just like you! I am filled with power!

The Spirit of Knowledge

You have given me more understanding than those who teach me,
for I've absorbed your eye-opening revelation.

Psalm 119:99

God, I long to walk in the fullness of your knowledge. I am not content with what I know or with what others have taught me. I want revelation that I cannot learn from anyone but you. I ask that you would pour out the Spirit of Knowledge upon me.

Open my eyes, let me see the way you see. Feed me with each word that flows from your mouth. Give me dreams, visions, angelic visitations and fill me with your revelation knowledge. Whisper secrets to my heart and unveil mysteries of things to come. All glory, power, knowledge, wisdom, and revelation are yours.

Let the light of your revelation burn into my being. Enlighten the eyes of my heart and may golden nuggets of never-before-discovered truth fall upon my soul.

The Spirit of the Fear of the Lord

But still one question remains:
How do I live in the holy fear of God?
Show me the right path to take.

Psalm 25:12

Awaken my heart with the Spirit of the Fear of the Lord. Ignite my soul with holy awe that drives me to my knees. I will worship you with pure devotion when I catch even a glimpse of your divine majesty. Your presence leaves me undone.

You are the Lion and the Lamb, perfected beauty and uncontaminated wisdom. The alluring mystery of your glory both intrigues and overwhelms me. I grow weak as I draw near. Give me grace to endure the purity and holiness that streams from your being—it is more than I can bear.

You are a consuming, living flame. Every fiber of my being is completely captivated as the awakening power of your Spirit falls upon me. Because of the anointing of your presence that I carry within me, other hearts will turn to you with holy abandon.

Your love has freed me from unrighteous fears, but I welcome the Spirit of the Fear of the Lord.

Arise and Shine

They will tell the world of the lavish splendor of your kingdom
and preach about your limitless power.
They will demonstrate for all to see your miracles of might
and reveal the glorious majesty of your kingdom.

Psalm 145:11–12

God, your love is contagious and I cannot help but share it. Your Word is like a fire blazing through my bones—I cannot hold it back. As a citizen of heaven, you've called me to release the atmosphere of heaven everywhere I go. You chose me to go into the world and represent you well. With love and compassion, I will set people free.

What mighty miracles you did when you walked upon the earth! Now you've passed the baton to me. You said that I would do even greater works than you did, and with your Holy Spirit living inside of me, I believe I can. I will not force the rules of religion down anyone's throat, but with love and power, I will introduce them to the reality of your kingdom.

I am the light of the world and the salt of the earth. Together we will open the eyes of the blind, turning them from darkness to light. In your name I will cast out demons, raise the dead, and lay hands on the sick and see them recover. I will speak what you tell me to say and pull the blessings of heaven to earth, because I am your child. I will arise and shine!

When You're Silent

O people of God, your time has come to quietly trust,
waiting upon the Lord now and forever.

Psalm 131:3

Lord, thank you for teaching me the beauty of silence. At times your presence comes swiftly and profoundly, surprising me with glorious encounters. Yet at other times, there is nothing but the stillness of being—just being—and I experience no manifestations of your glory. Now I understand how important these moments are and I'm learning to embrace every season.

In the quiet times, when I cannot sense you, I learn to love you for who you are. My faith rises within me and pours its truest devotion upon you with unselfish love. I seek only to bless you. I'm so grateful to you for these opportunities to honor you with a pure heart.

I won't despise the moments when you seem far away, when you lift the awareness of your presence. I know you have not really left. Though I desire your closeness and know you will unveil my heart again, I will lavish my worship upon you and wait with expectancy.

Being Me

*Your very hands have held me
and made me who I am;
give me more revelation-light
so I may learn to please you more.*

Psalm 119:73

Lord, when I'm with you, I discover who I truly am. You free me to be myself and enjoy being me. Though my heart is to honor you and please you always, I don't have to work for your love. I can simply live my life from the inside out and savor each day with you.

Truly alive, with your Spirit living in me, I believe I can and will fulfill my purpose on this earth. Nothing and no one could ever stop what you have set in motion. I am yours, completely. You empower me to live a life of holy determination. You breathe life into dormant dreams and cause me to hope.

Life has become fun again! I live with one goal in mind—to have my heart, soul, and mind so totally immersed in you that everything else flows from there. Love, joy, peace, patience, kindness, goodness, faithfulness, and self-control manifest easily when I remember who I truly am. My identity is established when I find myself in you.

Yearn

I overflow with praise when I come before you,
for the anointing of your presence satisfies me like nothing else.
You are such a rich banquet of pleasure to my soul.

Psalm 63:5

God, I'm not sure if I can describe these yearnings that grip my soul and drive me to my knees. I'm lovesick. Struck with unyielding desire for more of your holy presence. My very being is consumed with deep longing to know you more. It is like unrelenting fire trapped within the very marrow of my bones.

Your love blazes through the sky with each rising of the sun. It awakens my heart to seek you. Daily I will come into your presence with songs of praise. I will dance upon the failures of the past and wave my arms like banners, in celebration of all you've done. This holy passion is uncontainable. It overflows into every situation, exploding from my spirit with indescribable yearnings that can only be satisfied by your magnificent love.

You are a rich banquet of pleasure. As I delight in you, you manifest the fulfillment of my dreams. Lord, tear down the walls that hold me back from experiencing the deepest depths of your love. Awaken my soul to passionately pursue you forever.

Await

The earth quivers and quakes before you,
splitting open and breaking apart.
Now come and heal it, for it is shaken to its depths.

Psalm 60:2

God, sometimes it feels as though you're distant. As if you've deserted me and left me to drink the wine of bewilderment. But I know you're a good Father. You've given me miraculous signs of your love, even in the darkest valleys of my life. If there is a wall between us, it was not built by you.

The earth trembles, awaiting your return. Come. Put your love on display and draw me close again, for the lessons of life have been hard. There is no person alive who can give me the help I need.

In your sovereignty I heard you speak. Whether it boomed from the heavens or within the stillness of my heart, I'm not sure, but I heard you, nevertheless. You have not forgotten about me! You will measure out the portion of my inheritance and keep every promise. Your goodness is not held back. Though nations rise up against you, you will hold them in derision, for you are triumphant. You will bless the land and cause it to blossom once again.

Empower Me

My strength is found when I wait upon you.
Watch over me, God, for you are my Mountain Fortress;
you set me on high!

Psalm 59:9

God you are amazing! You're like a fortress set on top of a majestic mountain. Taking refuge in you isn't boring. I don't have to cower in some corner when my enemies are lurking about. I can run through the vast expanse of your halls and know I'm safe.

When I had nothing to cling to but you and could do nothing but wait for you to answer, you made me strong. You empowered me with your love and taught me patience. Now I know how to trample the enemy because I've seen you do it. With vivid displays of power, you scatter his camp and confuse his plans.

You are the Ruler of your people, the God-King over the entire earth. Victory is our portion when we walk with you, day by day. Your strength is my song of joy, and my lyrics of love are for all to hear. You are my Strength, my Stronghold, and my Savior—the Faithful One who greets me with love.

Measureless Grace

So here's what I've learned through it all:
Leave all your cares and anxieties at the feet of the Lord,
and measureless grace will strengthen you.

Psalm 55:22

Sometimes I just want to fly away. To ascend above the storm clouds and raging winds, straight into the shelter of your presence. For my heart is trembling and all I want to do is hide myself in your arms of love and cry. I can't see anything except this horror staring me in the face. People can be so cruel. It's bad enough when they despise me because they don't know me, but when it's an intimate friend, one who I've worshiped with side by side, it breaks my heart.

I reach for you and wait for your hand to quell the raging pain. You are enthroned through everlasting ages. I close my eyes and catch a glimpse of you. There you are, writing my story with strokes of love. Your friendship is unfailing and unchanging.

I listen beyond the noise and find the sound of life streaming from your voice. Measureless grace strengthens me. Anxiety and disappointment glide easily from my shoulders and I lay them at your feet. Your peace will forever be my portion.

The Invitation

Purify my conscience! Make this leper clean again!
Wash me in your love until I am pure in heart.

Psalm 51:7

God, I invite you into the hidden places of my heart, so we can face my corruption together. I'm done hiding. Done living in shame. Done pretending. Go straight into the darkest crevice of my soul and illuminate it with your presence, so that not even a shadow of sin exists. I know your abundant love is enough to wash away my iniquities. Purify every part of me.

I want nothing to do with sin—great or small. I'll not excuse self-motives or bad attitudes. No longer will I pretend I have my act together on the outside, when the inside is polluted. The sting of hurting our relationship is too painful for me to do anything other than throw myself at your mercy and embrace your loving compassion.

Create a new, clean heart within me. Fill me with pure thoughts and holy desires, so my life will please you fully. Then my song of joy will return. You are the passion of my life. There is nothing more satisfying than living face-to-face with you.

Sacred Oil

But I am like a flourishing olive tree,
anointed in the house of God.
I trust in the unending love of God;
his passion toward me is forever and ever.

Psalm 52:8

Lord, I want to live a life that is pleasing to you—a life of gratitude and grace. May my heart be one with yours forever. I know that this life of covenant blessing cannot be earned by anything I do, but I want to honor you by always choosing what's good and right in your sight.

I've seen the path of the wicked—those who are great in their own eyes, untouchable and accountable to no one but themselves. Theirs is a dark and lonely path. They harm everyone around them and boast in the trouble they cause. They are poor, wretched individuals, in need of your love. We are all searching, all trying to find our way. But only when we draw near to you will we flourish like an olive tree, flowing with sacred oil.

I too am in constant need of your love. I rely on it. Your never-ending passion toward me keeps me on the path that leads to you. It is like walking on the blossoms of your breath, your beautiful name spilling from my lips.

Light

For you have saved my soul from death
and my feet from stumbling
so that I can walk before the Lord
bathed in his life-giving light.

Psalm 56:13

Bathe me in your light, so every part of me is permeated with your splendor. I want to walk with you in glory, right here on earth. I want to live in union with you, so I know what's on your heart. I want to know you more than anyone has ever known you before.

I'm reaching for your goodness—nothing can hold it back. Come and be with me; let me feel you by my side. Walk with me in the cool of the day and the storms of night. You've always been so good to me. You're my closest Friend.

Your love never runs dry. It is a well of promise and I draw from its depths. It pours over me in times of joy, in times when I'm stripped to the bone. Everything about you is lovely. All I know and have yet to discover brings light to my soul.

Remember

But then I remember that you, O Lord,
still sit enthroned as King over all!
The fame of your name will be revealed to every generation!
Psalm 102:12

Lord, I don't know what happened. Everything seemed to be going great and then all of a sudden my happiness went up in smoke. The days that were once flooded with blessing are now consumed by trials—one after the other. Everyone thinks I'm holding up under the pressure, but I'm not. Without your help, I'll never get through this.

That's the answer, isn't it? To remember that you are the same King who has helped me through dark seasons many times before. To shake off the despair that the enemy planned to destroy me with and fill the atmosphere with praise, instead of this incessant crying and complaining.

I don't know how long it will take for you to manifest the answer to my prayers, but you will. My story will have a happy ending. You will restore me and refresh me with your breath from heaven. I close my eyes and you still my heart. I begin to see things from your perspective. You haven't abandoned me. You are faithful.

May

Shout

Sing your songs tuned to his glory!
Tell the world how wonderful he is.

Psalm 66:2

Today I want to shout, so the whole world knows how amazing you are! Everyone everywhere must know what it's like to be the child of the King. Though trials come and difficult seasons seem to strip us of strength, you uphold us, you never leave us. We emerge better than we were before, because of your faithfulness.

If everyone knew you the way I do, they would understand why I can't stay quiet. If they would take just a moment to pause in your presence and allow you to open their eyes, they would never be the same. All the earth would bow before you in worship and join me in singing your glories. It would take their breath away.

You hold our lives safely in your hands. No heart goes unnoticed. When we turn to you, you visit us with words of love that awaken our hearts. You watch every movement of every nation. You are great and powerful working miracles from generation to generation. How I long to see the day when the world finally surrenders to your love.

Unrelenting Mercy

How I wish their time of rescue were already here
and that God would appear,
arising from the midst of his Zion-people
to save and restore his very own.

Psalm 14:7

You are a God of restoration. Your searching gaze goes forth in full pursuit, looking for those whose withering souls grope in darkness. Though they reach for what cannot satisfy, your mercy rushes in. The smoldering flames of once-impassioned hearts draw you like a bee to honey. You will restore those with only the faintest flicker of hope.

Gently turn the faces of those who have lost their way, so they can see you once again. Rise in their midst and appear before them. Bathe the weary souls with your Spirit. Reignite the flames of passion that once burned bright. Heal them, for they have fallen prey to the enemy's schemes.

In you, the weak are not disqualified nor despised. Instead, you lift them up with unrelenting mercy. Your zealous devotion will never fail. Your faithful love will find a way.

Our Safe Place

Keep me safe, O mighty God.
I run for dear life to you, my Safe Place.

Psalm 16:1

Lord, you are my safe place. Hide me under the shadow of your wings. When everything around me is shaking, you are my sure foundation. Silence the fears that threaten my sanity. Deliver me from mind-sets that are contrary to your Word. I have nowhere to run, but you.

You speak light into the darkest places. Even the orphans and the oppressed will no longer be terrified when you fulfill their hopes. Tenderly, you care for the fatherless and will not forever ignore the needs of the poor. All who trust in you will never be alone. You are our Helper—the One who holds us when we're weak.

Thank you for your presence which continually surrounds me. Your words, engraved into my heart, are my constant meditation. They sustain me and remind me of your mighty protection. Danger may crash all around me, to my right and left, but I will be unharmed. I will not be intimidated. I won't even flinch, for you are by my side!

Don't Pass Me By

Then he broke through and transformed all my wailing
into a whirling dance of ecstatic praise!
He has torn the veil and lifted from me
the sad heaviness of mourning.
He wrapped me in the glory-garments of gladness.

Psalm 30:11

Answer me, God. I don't know what to do. Let your voice be louder than my doubts. Cause my heart to sing again. I have nothing to offer you but the yes in my heart. Don't let the flickering flame of hope be snuffed out. Flood my soul with wisdom.

I sit and wait in silence, leaning into the seemingly insignificant faith I have left. Don't pass me by.

Before you now, in this place of rest, your presence permeates every fiber of my being. My tears of fear are dried by the breath of love. Suddenly, you reach out and tear the veil; the heaviness of mourning is lifted and I can see again. The path before me, once obscured by looming shadows, comes clearly into view.

I've believed for so long, but now I see the promises. The answer is so clear. It was there all along, held safely in your hands. All I needed to do was to rest. Now you've turned my sadness into a whirling dance of ecstatic praise! I will shout it from the mountains—you are faithful!

The Perfect Plan

I hear the Lord saying, "I will stay close to you,
instructing and guiding you along the pathway for your life.
I will advise you along the way
and lead you forth with my eyes as your guide."

Psalm 32:8

Lord, I'm not sure where you're taking me. I've not been down this road before. There are obstacles as far as I can see. I'm not sure I'm ready. Remember the cleft of the rock, where you hid me before? Or the resting place of your chambers where you refreshed my soul? Let's go back there!

I see the excitement in your face. I feel your hand securely holding mine. You lean in and whisper assurances to my heart. "Trust me," you say.

My heart beats wildly in my chest. You have never failed me before and though I'm more nervous than excited, I squeeze your hand and you lead me on.

Life with you is never as I've planned. It is filled with both storms that rage and breezes that refresh. The only thing I can be sure of is that you are the Lord over it all. Nothing else matters, as long as I'm with you. In the end, everything will turn out right.

My entire life has led me to this one point—I am yours and you are mine. From the very beginning, that was always your perfect plan.

Unending Love

Drink deeply of the pleasures of this God.
Experience for yourself the joyous mercies he gives
to all who turn to hide themselves in him.

Psalm 34:8

Your freedom is so liberating! A gift I don't deserve. Over and over your mercy lifts me up. When I feel distant and forsaken, you recalibrate my heart so it beats in rhythm with yours, once again.

How beautiful your love is! Always giving, with no demands for reciprocation. Humble. Engraved within your very nature. I want to hide myself here, in your embrace, and forever drink deeply of this love. I can never get enough.

You see my humanity and the many times I fail, yet with relentless pursuit, you cheer me on. You smear the pages of sin with holy blood, so I cannot read its once raging accusation. Inspired by your kindness, I run to pursue my dreams and leave the past far behind. This is who I truly am—your child, your protégé, the one you know by name.

This is unending love—the story of life with you.

Unshakable

The Almighty is alive and conquers all!
Praise is lifted high to the unshakable God!
Towering over all, my Savior-God is worthy to be praised!

Psalm 18:46

Yᴏu are unshakable. A heavenly tower of strength for all who abide within. Your path is perfect; your promises have proven true. You are the favor that clothes me and the power that makes me strong.

Your gentleness has brought me back to life. Your love surprises me. Out of the ashes you discovered unexpected beauty. My once dry and dusty soul now flows with rivers of living water. My fears are silenced by your love.

Dressed in clouds of mystery, you hold me tight. Your glory ignites my faith, yet renders me speechless. How mighty you are! You hold nothing back from me. Your passion is stronger than death. Your power is limitless.

Today, I step into victory. You have restored my roar and made me great. You are worthy to be praised!

The Testing

Keep trusting in the Lord and do what is right in his eyes.
Fix your heart on the promises of God and you will be secure,
feasting on his faithfulness.

Psalm 37:3

God, perfect me in your love, so I lack nothing. My faith is being tested. I'm weary to the bone, yet I embrace this trial as an opportunity for my character to grow. I will not be defeated by the looming fears. I refuse to sink in a mire of self-pity. I will fix my heart on your promises, for you are the fuel that ignites my praise.

Pour out the beauty of your faithfulness upon my life. Help me to do what is right in your sight, and reach for me when I start to lose my grip. When circumstances become a whirling storm of dust and I cannot see, wash me in your cleansing waters and heal my vision.

This current trial will become my future strength. Each day I will seek your face and you will anchor me in your love. Your faithfulness never fails, regardless of the path it takes to get to me.

Wondrous Love

This is just too wonderful, deep, and incomprehensible!
Your understanding of me brings me wonder and strength.

Psalm 139:6

You know everything there is to know about me. My strengths and weaknesses, my hopes and fears—there is nothing hidden that you don't see. Yet with all of the things that your truth reveals, you still call me lovely. You believe in me even when I don't believe in myself.

Your grace and compassion are too profound for words. I live in continual awe because of your relentless love. It knows no bounds. It always forgives. When all I see is darkness, you find the tiniest speck of light and declare it more dazzling than the sun. What a wonderful and encouraging Friend you are. It's impossible to exaggerate your goodness.

Your uplifting love brings me strength and causes me to soar! You've brought meaning to my life, and you've won my heart. I will hold nothing back.

Lean In

God, there's just no one like you;
there's no other god as famous as you.
You outshine all others and your miracles
make it easy to know you.

Psalm 86:8

I won't push myself to praise you. I will simply step into the reality of your love and exist fully within each movement of your heart. I bow before you and surrender my soul—that is all that you require. You have already paved the way to your presence. There is no striving to find your love. I just lean into your grace. You make it easy to know you.

I was made for love. Created to live in perfect union and constant communion with you. Your love outshines all others. No one holds my heart as tenderly and carefully as you do. You are the love that stepped out of eternity, just to save me. You are the God of mystery. You have mended my broken soul.

No longer am I restless, because you have given me rest—this is the power to overcome. Amazing grace has set me free.

Incarnate

I know your power and presence shines on all your lovers.
Your glory always hovers over all who bow low before you.

Psalm 85:9

Shine the light of your dazzling splendor upon my life. Empower me with courage as I bow before your majesty. Strengthen me with endurance to last a lifetime. Storms come and go, but my will remains steadfast—anchored in you.

Pour your grace upon my heart. Hover over me as I yield all to you. Come with your glory. Let me enjoy it, feel it, and never push it away by trying to make sense of something so holy. I will embrace you without reservation, the same way you have embraced me.

You are the first and the last and everything in between. Much greater than my understanding, you are the God of mystery. You are the still small voice that whispers to me from deep within. There is no denying your power and grace. You gave it all for me—the wonder of love incarnate.

Unwavering

Why would I fear the future?
For I'm being pursued only by your goodness and unfailing love.
Psalm 23:6

God, I feel the waves of your love crashing upon my soul. The undercurrent of your love is pulling me in. I know I shouldn't fight it. Help me to relax and allow you to take me wherever you desire, no matter how scary it seems at times.

I want the kind of faith that moves mountains—unwavering and brave. I know I was born into victory when I stepped into you, but at times I'm overwhelmed by the giants in the land. Some of the things you ask me to do seem far too outlandish. Forgive me for my unbelief. Give me eyes that see with your perspective. Pursue me with your goodness and unfailing love. Have mercy on me!

I release my anxieties about what tomorrow holds. I want to live my life in the blessing of now and surrender the future into your hands, without constantly trying to understand it. The revelation of *grace for today* is enough. I will rest in your kindness and trust in your unfailing love.

Nothing Compares

Just one day of intimacy with you is like
a thousand days of joy rolled into one!
I'd rather stand at the threshold in front of the Gate Beautiful,
ready to go in and worship my God,
than to live my life without you
in the most beautiful palace of the wicked.

Psalm 84:10

God, the most extravagant longings of my heart cannot be satisfied by anyone but you. You are my strength, my motivation, my reason for living. Tether me to your love. Your kindness has led me to repentance. Wrap me in your arms and look me in the eye—nothing is hidden from you.

Your presence is a shield of protection around me—I will rest there always. Thank you for your gift of grace. For filling me with relentless desire to know you. I'd rather stand at the gate that leads to you, than to stand in beautiful palaces apart from you. Nothing compares to being near you. No one can match your power. No one rivals your love.

Fill my life with the brilliance of your glory. Illuminate my paths with your radiant splendor, so I will never lose my way. I lack nothing when I'm with you. You provide more than enough. Your faithfulness is euphoric; you never fail me. God, you are the answer to every prayer and I will trust you forever.

Israel, the Apple of Your Eye

Our enemies keep saying,
"Now is the time to wipe Israel off the map.
We'll destroy even the memory of her existence!"

Psalm 83:4

God, enemies conspire against your cherished ones. They want to wipe Israel off the map. Your beloved, the apple of your eye, needs your intervention. Guide your people into truth and redeem your holy land from corruption. The enemies of Israel are our enemies too. I stand today and pray for peace to flood the land.

Bring an end to violence and suffering, let justice prevail. Let your kingdom come and rule the land. God of Abraham, Isaac, and Jacob, envelop Israel in your shalom. Let all of her enemies be pushed back, blown away like tumbleweeds in a windstorm.

Answer the cries streaming from your Promised Land. Show them your faithfulness and grant them salvation. Then the sounds of rejoicing—unquenchable like the roar of a mighty flame—will be heard in the streets. When Israel blossoms, the whole world will be filled with fruit. You alone are Yahweh, the Most High God exalted over all the earth!

Fill Me

*"I will feed you with my spiritual bread.
You will feast and be satisfied with me
feeding on my revelation-truth like honey
dripping from the cliffs of the high place."*

Psalm 81:16

Father, you are my God; there is no other. I will worship you from the depths of my spirit and never take your love for granted again. Your mercy is so beautiful to me. When I lived according to my selfish fantasies, I was miserable—always grasping for something to feed my ego. All it took was surrendering my stubborn heart and yielding to your lordship. Then I tasted what life with you was like and I will never turn back.

Give me grace to faithfully follow your footsteps. Empower me to live my days before you with an undivided heart. You have delivered me from bondage. When I open my mouth to speak, fill it with the truth of your Word and let every promise come to pass. Your revelation is sweeter than honey.

Feed my spirit with spiritual bread that satisfies my greatest hunger. Let me feast upon your presence. Thank you for your mercy—for understanding my struggles and unveiling the work of your Spirit in me.

Set Apart

*"Because I love him and treasure him,
my faithfulness will always protect him.
I will place my great favor upon him,
and I will cause his power and fame to increase."*

Psalm 89:24

Lord, I feel your great power surrounding me. Like David of old, I am sustained by your grace, anointed by the oil of your Spirit. You are my Father and strong Savior. I overcome whatever I face, because you have destined me for victory. Your covenant is an unbreakable promise—I trust in it fully.

Lift me higher and higher, until I soar on the wings of favor. Set me apart to be a gracious dispenser of your glory. I honor you and bow before your marvelous splendor, knowing that without you I am nothing. Though power and fame may set me before kings and queens, my success is found in *your* triumph.

I owe everything to you. You are astounding—the only standard for truth. Not even the mighty angels compare to you. You outshine us all with glory that reaches to the sky, yet you have chosen to manifest yourself through imperfect vessels. King of Glory, I rejoice in your unceasing grace and astounding blessing upon my life.

No Holding Back

Everyone come meet his face with a thankful heart!
Don't hold back your praises;
make him great by your shouts of joy!

Psalm 95:2

God, I'm not sure whether to kneel in reverence, honoring you as the mighty God, or to wildly celebrate you as Creator. When I think about how great you are, my heart soars.

At times, my joy is uncontainable, and at other times, I'm so overwhelmed by your majesty I can barely stand. One moment, I'm dancing and singing your praise, and the next, I'm prostrate before your throne. In one hand, you hold the mysteries of the whole world, and in the other, the world itself.

I cannot refrain from proclaiming your greatness. If everyone truly understood how magnificent you are, they would dedicate themselves to you, wholeheartedly. I pray my passion would be contagious, Father, so everyone would join me in praising you.

I am thoroughly convinced of your power and love. With untamed praise and deepest reverence, I will honor you eternally.

Light in the Darkness

At each and every sunrise I will awake to do what's right
and put to silence those who love wickedness,
freeing God's people from their evil grip.
I will do all of this because of my great love for you!

Psalm 101:8

Lord, when you examine my life, I pray you will find integrity, honor, and compassion as the theme. I live in a world of corruption, where anything goes and righteous standards are frowned upon. Let it not be so in my family. For generations to come, may we be an example of wisdom and love for others to follow.

I will choose to keep the pure and godly as my closest friends, but help me to never be prideful or shun anyone. Though I will not be named among the wicked, let my kindness attract them. When they look to me for counsel and support, anoint me to speak from a heart of compassion, with words of godly wisdom. May I shine with the glory of your Spirit within me to a world smoldering in darkness and desperate for your touch.

The deepest cry of my heart is to live a life that reflects you into the world around me. May I walk humbly with you all of my days and see this passionate pursuit of godliness continue for generations.

Entirely Yours

*You're so kind and tenderhearted to those who
don't deserve it and so very patient with people
who fail you! Your love is like a flooding river
overflowing its banks with kindness.*

Psalm 103:8

I was thinking today about how merciful you've been to me. How in spite of all I've done, you kissed my heart with forgiveness. You rescued me from hell and saved my life. When I lost sight of you and ran around in circles feeling alone and confused, you rushed to my side. I don't deserve your tenderhearted love and I don't understand your patience, but I'm thankful for both.

I dedicate myself to you. With all of my heart, I pray there will never be any part of me that is not entirely yours. I want to live a life of celebration, never forgetting your miracle of kindness. You have satisfied my deepest desires with the substance of your love. Sometimes this crown that you've placed on my head feels too big, but I accept the honor of representing you in the earth. I bow before you in wonder—my whole life surrendered to you.

Genius

O Lord, what an amazing variety of all you have created!
Wild and wonderful is this world you have made,
while wisdom was there at your side!
This world is full of so many creatures, yet each belongs to you!
Psalm 104:24

My heart is stirred with praise. Sweet thoughts of you flow as I ponder your movement within creation. Your provision is astounding—a medley of supply. Your diversity is revealed throughout nature. Every creature, great and small, has its place in your design.

I praise you for the earth you made for us, held together by your great wisdom: springs cascade through the rocky streams; our thirst is continually quenched with rain from heaven; the mountains rise at your command; and the seas are tethered by your word.

The complexity of the body fascinates me. How intricately you have woven me together, how meticulously you have fashioned me in your image. You're a genius! This body, this vessel where imperfect people harbor imperfect thoughts, is the place you call your temple. It seems an impossible circumstance.

Father, you are the source of my joy. With blissful shouts of hallelujah, I will declare your praise! What a wild and wonderful world you have made.

Your Masterpiece

Compared to all this cosmic glory,
why would you bother with puny, mortal man
or be infatuated with Adam's sons?

Psalm 8:4

I'm mesmerized; awestruck over the beauty of your creation. The evidence of your creative genius streams from the heavens with glory. All of earth echoes your name. There is no denying that you are the Master Artist who set before us your most beautiful works of art.

The moon and stars are dazzling, brilliantly glowing against the night sky like jewels mounted in their settings. Still, I'm awed by something even more splendid than the wonders I see above. God, though you're famous—great and powerful—you know me by name and call me your child. I am your masterpiece.

My Father, whose name is known throughout the universe, you have created me to be just like you. Filled with glory, I'll shine in the darkness, illuminating the world with your splendor and compassion. Crowned with majesty, I'll stand in authority before wild animals and magnificent mountains.

What an honor it is to know you and be known by you. Together, we fill the earth with the nature of who you are—the very essence of love.

The Beautiful Path

For you bring me a continual revelation
of resurrection life, the path to the bliss
that brings me face-to-face with you.

Psalm 16:11

What great love is this, which so profoundly surrounds me and leaves me utterly undone? It is you, Lord—my portion, my prize, and my delight—the One I have chosen over all others.

Every moment of my life, you are here. I'm totally and completely secure in your unfathomable love. You continually reveal the overwhelming privilege of following you—a beautiful path of resurrection life on which I am honored to travel. I trust in you with full abandon. My destiny is safe in your hands.

You counsel and correct me with such wisdom, I'm left with no rebuttal—only a deep sense of awe and humility, which compels me to praise you with lifted hands and surrendered heart.

In the night you whisper words that fall upon my heart like costly jewels. So precious is your love for me. Even while I sleep and my body rests securely in your presence, my heart and soul explode with praise. You are my eternal and exquisite joy.

When Friends Turn against Me

My love for you has my heart on fire!
My passion consumes me for your house!
Nothing will turn me away. Even though people hate me and
insult me for loving you, I know they hate you even more.

Psalm 69:9

Lord, I'm heartbroken. Friends have become enemies all because of my love for you. They mock, curse, and insult me. Some have even threatened me. They want nothing to do with me anymore, unless I stop talking about you. But I'll never do that! My love for you has inflamed my heart. You're my reason for living. I have nothing against them, but I certainly won't choose them over you when they're the ones putting conditions on their love. You've never done that to me. Your love is eternal. You loved me before I ever loved you.

I've never been so hurt. But I suppose you know how it feels. They hate you even more than they hate me. I don't want to become a stumbling block to them—to somehow confuse them by my actions. I've tried telling them you haven't demanded that I live this way. I'm just consumed by uncontainable passion, but they only laugh.

Lord, turn your heart to me. Let me see your face. If you will come and answer this one prayer, all of my pain will be worth it. Come with your love and be my Best Friend.

All I Need

You lead me with your secret wisdom.
And following you brings me into
your brightness and glory!

Psalm 73:24

Lord, thank you for your infinite mercy and grace. So often I get stuck in my head, wasting time trying to understand matters that are too difficult for me—things which only make sense with your wisdom. It's not possible to be led by my spirit when I let my mind take control. I only end up complaining about things and feeling miserable. If it weren't for your compassion, I'd never find peace.

Yet, in spite of my whining, you draw me close and comfort me with your counsel. Your kindness opens my eyes, so I can see again. Forgive me for trying to analyze every finite detail of life instead of trusting you with the sheer abandon of a child. Nothing in the whole world compares to you. Your love is all I ever need.

The glory of your presence protects me. You whisper secrets that calm my raging thoughts. You anoint me with peace. I don't have to understand everything. I only have to stay near you—coming closer and closer until imaginations are illuminated by your truth. This is the place of joy. This is life with you.

Deluge

God, you are so resplendent and radiant!
Your majesty shines from your everlasting mountain.
Nothing could be compared to you in glory!

Psalm 76:4

Father, you are holy—unlike anyone in the entire world. I stand in awe of your brilliance, struck silent by your splendor. Your love is like a waterfall, unceasingly tumbling upon my life, washing away the debris of worldly pursuits. Refresh me—over and over again—with this deluge of sacred affection until I am free of the clamor that screams within.

Shine your majesty from your everlasting mountain, so all will see it. I want everyone to know what it's like to live in the awestruck wonder of your glory. Those who don't know you will be forever changed—there's no denying your magnificence. Even the mightiest of men will become paralyzed by your presence, but when they come to, they'll be better off.

Don't hold back, Lord! Stun the world, shake things up a bit, and get their attention. Roar your rebuke if you must. I'll be flat on my face worshiping you, but I'm sure it would be quite a sight—seeing the earth hold its breath as they discover the glorious truth.

My Righteous King

Regal power surrounds [Yahweh]
as he sits securely on his throne.
He's in charge of it all, the entire world,
and he knows what he's doing!

Psalm 93:1

God, you are holy; the one true King who rules heaven and earth in majestic splendor. You are a Tower of Strength for all who run to you for protection. You condemn the plots of wickedness; the sound of your voice stills the chaos of catastrophe.

Yahweh, you have reigned from eternity past to eternity future with judgments that are pure and right. Send forth your royal decrees of righteousness for all the world to hear. Teach us your ways and ignite our hearts with passion to follow you. As your cherished ones, illuminate us with revelation so we'll reflect your brilliance to the world around us.

Even in the darkest season of my soul, I will cling to you and embrace the lessons you teach, for even the sting of your correction is sweet. Examine my every thought as I yield myself to your lordship. Your dominion and authority abides forever. You are my righteous King.

Our Great God

Mountains melt away like wax in a fire
when the Lord of all the earth draws near!
Psalm 97:5

Witnessing your power is both wonderful and terrifying. Those who don't know you are left wide-eyed, as they tremble before you. Your foes try to run and hide, but they are consumed by your blazing glory before they can move an inch. Even the mountains melt like wax as you draw near. Those who have pushed you aside to serve other gods try to cover themselves from your glory, but your mercy reaches into their darkest shame and sets them free.

And then there's us—your lovers who join all of heaven in declaring your majesty. We witness your glory in the sky and worship you with unveiled faces. You fill us with joy greater than the world has ever known. What an honor it is to declare your ways and shout your praise.

Lord, release the harvest of souls who are gasping and groaning, desperately searching for something to fill their empty lives. Awaken their hearts. Breathe your love upon them, so they will despise their pride and flourish in the radiance of your splendor.

Refresh Us

Yahweh is King over all!
Everyone trembles in awe before him!
He rules enthroned between the wings
of the cherubim. So let the earth shake
and quake in wonder before him!

Psalm 99:1

You, Lord, are great and glorious, enthroned between the wings of the cherubim where you rule. Through pillars of clouds, you speak and instruct. Reveal your love and awaken our hearts. It would be impossible for those who experience the reality of your touch, not to respond. Perhaps a torrent of praise would erupt and cause the earth to shake beneath my feet! Or, we would find everyone facedown before your throne of glory.

I wonder what it would be like if the nations truly saw how magnificent you are. If they witnessed how perfectly you rule, I'm sure they would become lovers of justice as well. One day they will proclaim your glorious nature and great forgiveness. They will turn to you in full surrender.

Pour out the reality of your splendor. Refresh humanity by diffusing the greatness of your power and love into every darkened crevice of our existence.

Constant One

God's heavenly throne is eternal, secure, and strong,
and his kingdom rules the entire universe!
Psalm 103:19

Lord, I praise you for your everlasting faithfulness to those who follow your ways and keep your Word. Throughout the generations, you have kept every gracious promise you've made. Though our lives are but fleeting moments upon the earth, your love extends throughout eternity. You are mindful of us, caring for us even more intensely than a loving father with his children.

I want to be one of your messengers of power. One of the hidden and precious gems within your treasure chest. I want to shine with the facet of your likeness that no one else has—to leave behind a legacy of endless love that reaches into every facet of society.

Your throne is eternal, secure, and strong. You rule the entire universe, yet your devotion to your beloved is unrelenting—you know us inside and out. Thank you for your mercy, which overcomes all the messes we make. I bow before you in reverent awe. In you we lack nothing. You are the constant one.

Stillness

Let me feel your tender love for I am yours.
Give me more understanding of your wonderful ways.

Psalm 119:124

Lord, you're beautiful. I'm lovesick for you, yearning to hear your tender words of wisdom and truth. I feel you drawing me closer to you and I will come. All distractions out of reach, I close my eyes and turn my heart to you. I want to see you.

Stillness. At times nothing more than the peace that floods my being. No voice. You speak no answer to the many questions I have asked. You show me no snapshots of revelation. Only the ordained unity of my body, soul, and spirit.

This is what I needed—just to be with you. To lie back in your arms and rest. My mind quiet. My heart overcome by the peace of your presence. All is well. You are in control. You love me.

Until I Found You

How long will you set your heart on shadows,
chasing your lies and delusions?

Psalm 4:2

God, you are my righteousness—the One I have chosen to live for. It wasn't until I yielded my ways for yours that I discovered how beautifully you could pull it all together. You don't need my endless striving; you only need my heart.

Like so many others before me, I didn't know what I was searching for until I found you. I was led astray by illusions of grandeur—my heart set on shadows. Now that you have come to me with your redeeming power, my spirit cries for those still chasing lies and delusions. Strip away the veil that obscures their sight and reveal yourself to them, Lord.

When others withdraw, I will follow after you. I will not pull back when things get hard. Though obstacles threaten to block the path that leads to you, you will light the way. Your love is never failing, ever patient. You're the victory that overcomes.

June

Seeds of Light

[God] sows seeds of light within his lovers,
and seeds of joy burst forth for the lovers of God!

Psalm 97:11

There are so many times when I can do nothing but fall prostrate before you—overwhelmed by emotion, at a loss for words. So often I refer to you as Father, and in truth, that's who you are to me. But then I'm struck with the realization that this One I call Father is also Yahweh, the King who reigns over all, and all I want to do is worship you.

As I gaze upon your face, I'm left with wobbly legs that feel too weak to hold me up. Knowing you as the God whose eyes flash with blazing glory-fire is much different than knowing you as Father and Friend. The seeds of light that you have sown within me seem to explode my soul—I cannot do anything more than surrender all to you.

The cares of this life, the fears and the distractions, disappear in this place of unrestrained passion. This is the place of freedom where shackles are undone and I can fly with you.

Sovereign

Praise forever Jehovah God, the God of Israel! ...
The blazing glory of his name will be praised forever!
May all the earth overflow with his glory!
Faithful is our King! Amen!

Psalm 72:18–19

I bless you, Lord! You are my Savior and my King. The One who reigns with perfect wisdom and justice. Pour out your kindness and compassion, so all who taste of it will trust in your great name. Blaze your way through chaos and corruption—make your way known.

Send reviving rain upon every city and countryside. Awaken the hearts of those who sleepwalk through life, wandering restlessly. Bless us so that we may be a blessing to others. Let the praises of your people be heard throughout the world, from generation to generation. May your light annihilate the hierarchies of darkness and illuminate our souls.

May your sovereignty be honored by kings in every land, as they yield their authority to you. The fame of your name springs forth from the lips of all who put their trust in you. God of wonders, you surpass our every expectation. Peace and prosperity are found in your kingdom and all who live there will never be put to shame. We will honor you as our faithful King forever.

Where I Belong

My heart, O God, is quiet and confident.
Now I can sing with passion your wonderful praises!
Psalm 57:7

I hear you speaking in the stillness of my heart. My mind has quieted and my faith is secure. You are here with me and in this place of peace, nothing else matters.

Too often my mind flutters in different directions, leading me away from you. But I'm learning, Lord. I won't let these little foxes steal from me any longer. I choose you. This is where I belong—in the place where every part of me is consumed with the reality of your holy presence.

Your nearness is intoxicating. Your peace is all-consuming. I feel as if I'm standing barefoot in a wide open field with soft grass beneath my feet, a gentle breeze lifting my hair, and the warm sun melting away confusion. I never want to leave. I want to remain in the silence of its uncluttered comfort.

I've decided I won't leave. I won't allow my mind to lead where my heart doesn't want to go. I will plant myself firmly in your love and make it my constant meditation. Even when fires are burning all around me, passionate praise will lead me back to you.

Author and Finisher of My Faith

You keep every promise you've ever made to me!
Since your love for me is so constant and endless,
I ask you, Lord, to finish every good thing
that you've begun in me!

Psalm 138:8

Daily I walk along the path of choosing. Decisions of life and death constantly before me. My choices will either draw me to you or lead me away. Each day I will declare that you are my God and nothing, not even my own selfish desires, will rule my life.

I fall into your arms. Not because I'm weary or defeated, but because I know you are my only hope. You don't want me to strive and take control. You only ask that I rest in you and release every care.

Without you, I'm nothing. Though my mind seeks to know the outcome of every situation, I will trust you. Your love has never failed me. I don't need to understand all of your plans, I only need to believe that they are good. You are the Author and Finisher of my faith. Every one of your faithful promises will come to pass. You will finish the work you've started in me.

Convey

God give me grace to guard my lips
from speaking what is wrong.
Psalm 141:3

God, have mercy on me and give me grace! Help me to guard my lips, so I don't hurt others with my words and sin against you. Teach me when to speak and when to stay silent. My words hold the power for life or death—may I always choose wisely.

I want to be quick to listen, slow to speak, and slow to anger. Let everything I say be seasoned with grace and love. When I need to speak a word of correction or rebuke, show me how to do it in a way that still makes the person feel valued and important. I only want to speak words that build up and never tear down. I will stay humble and esteem others the way you esteem me.

I was created in your image—to do and say things that look and sound like you. The mighty power of my words bring things into reality, so help me to only say things that agree with your Word. Let my words flow with goodness and kindness, streaming from a heart that is pure. May every word I speak be a blessing to those who hear it.

Theme

God, now that I'm old and gray, don't walk away.
Give me grace to demonstrate to the next generation
all your mighty miracles and your excitement
to show them your magnificent power!

Psalm 71:18

Your faithfulness has been the theme of my life. From the time I was little, you've been with me. Your love has sustained me, even in my darkest valleys. Your arms have held me when I clung to you for dear life. Even now, I hide myself in you, knowing you are the only safe place.

Thank you for the countless times you've been there for me. Without you, I would not have made it on this journey. I praise you for all you've done and all you will continue to do. Lord, stay close to me as I grow old and gray. Don't let me become feeble. Revive me. Anoint me to share what I know with this generation, so they will know that you and you alone are perfect—the only miracle-working God.

There's a harp in my heart and it flows with melodies of love to you.

A New Season

For God has given us these seasons of joy,
days that he decreed for us to celebrate and rejoice.

Psalm 81:4

Let the celebration begin! I will sing and dance to honor all you've done for me. The breakthrough felt so long in coming, but now I'm free. My heart was tested, my circumstances were filled with contention and mental slavery, but you didn't forget about me. From the place where mysteries hide, you came and saved me. You removed these back-breaking burdens and blessed the work of my hands. Thank you!

This marks a new season! What a relief to know that the strange time of suffering and affliction is over. It's almost too good to be true, but it isn't—it's just your faithfulness, Father. I'll embrace this time of joy with you and feast upon your goodness. God, you love a good party—I'll throw the biggest one! We will celebrate this amazing triumph, for you have turned seasons of weeping into seasons of joy. Thank you for all you've done!

Worthy

Everyone praise the Lord God of Israel,
always and forever!
For he is from eternity past
and will remain for the eternity to come.
That's the way it will be forever!
Faithful is our King! Amen!

Psalm 41:13

My faithful King, I honor you today. Mighty One, armed for battle and invincible in every way, you tower over all, yet choose to manifest through me. I will walk before you in integrity, your armor securely fastened around me, my enemies at my feet. You are the Lord God of Israel and the Commander of heaven's hosts.

I welcome you! The highest God—the only one worthy to be worshiped. You are my Savior and Glory-King who has appointed me as a king. May I one day grow into this crown you've placed upon my head.

You are from eternity past and will remain for eternity to come. You are ageless; the unshakeable God. Stories have been shared of all you've done—fables in the eyes of some— but I know you. You're my Father. My Creator. My healer. My Friend. The One who soars on the wings of spirit-wind and kisses me with life and love.

Crying Out

Yet when holy lovers of God cry out
to him with all their hearts,
the Lord will hear them and come to rescue
them from all their troubles.

Psalm 34:17

Lord, please silence the noise inside my head. I can't seem to find you through the storms of chaos and confusion. I'm reaching for you. Hoping for some relief from these non-stop questions that have spiraled out of control. Sometimes it feels as if I'm choking on dark clouds—barely breathing.

My heart is toward you and I'm facedown before your holy throne. Help me. Restore me with one touch of your mighty hand. Just whisper in my direction and it will be enough. I can't do this without you. I don't know how.

Quiet now. All striving gone. I simply wait for you.

All of a sudden, I feel you near. Love has stepped out of eternity. You have come. In my weakest moments you lift me with mercy and strengthen me with grace. I watch as the mountains, which cast shadows upon my soul, bow before your majesty. Shackles that once held me bound will become banners of praise, testifying of your faithful deliverance! Thank you for your inexhaustible love.

Quiet

The eyes of the Lord are upon
even the weakest worshipers who love him—
those who wait in hope and expectation
for the strong, steady love of God.

Psalm 33:18

I offer you my love. Though at times it's weak and my words are few, it's fueled by the deepest adoration. Come and wrap your arms of compassion around me. I'm waiting for you here, in the quiet of my soul. Waiting to rest my head upon your chest. Expecting your refreshing presence to touch me.

Your love is strong and steady—encouraging me when I'm beat down and exhausted. I want to offer you more than this, but it's all I can do to breathe and aim my worship in your direction.

I am so confident in our love. Even when I have nothing more to give than the yes in my heart, I know you still delight in me. All I want is to be with you. Lord, set your gaze upon my heart and see that every part of me is devoted to you. I hold nothing back. I am yours—eternally.

Reach

[God's people] turned away from faith and walked away in fear;
they failed to trust in his power to help them when he was near.
Still he spoke on their behalf and the skies opened up;
the windows of heaven poured out food,
the mercy bread-manna.
The grain of grace fell from the clouds.

Psalm 78:22–24

God, I need your mercy. Sometimes my faith is on fire and I have no problem believing you will come through. At other times fear screams so loudly that I waver and doubt.

I want my faith to please you—to so fully trust in your love for me that the greatest oppositions will not shake me. You are the foundation I have built my life upon; the core of my existence. When I fix my heart and mind upon you, you are the peace that surpasses all understanding. You are so full of grace and mercy that even when I am swayed by what is in front of me, you reach out your hand and steady me.

Though the enemy tries to persuade me to worry about what I cannot see, I choose to trust you and remind myself of your Word. I am not defeated, I am more than a conqueror because of you! I release all anxiety and fear of the unknown. Fill me with peace and joy as I wait expectantly for you.

Desire

What pleasure fills those who live every day in your temple,
enjoying you as they worship in your presence!
Psalm 84:4

Lord, I want to live every day in your temple—the place of your holy presence, where I come face-to-face with you. Within my heart is the highway that leads to you. Help me to never stray from it. Saturate my being as I worship and adore you. You are the source of true love, true contentment, and unrestrained joy.

By night fill my sleep with vibrant dreams. By day strengthen me and stay by my side. Even when my path winds through dark valleys filled with tears, I will build an altar and lay my pain before you. For you can heal, in one day, what would take a thousand elsewhere.

When you look at me, I pray that you will see beauty streaming from the lovesick longings of my soul. I desire nothing more than the overwhelming bliss of your nearness—constantly. May my declarations of love move your heart and pull you near. Ever nearer.

That All May Know

Don't stop! Keep on singing! Make his name famous!
Tell everyone every day how wonderful he is!
Give them the good news of our great Savior.
Take the message of his glory and miracles to every nation.
Tell them about all the amazing things he has done.

Psalm 96:2–3

Lord, everywhere I go I want to be an example of your compassion and power. It isn't enough for me to shout your praises—I must live life in a way that demonstrates your love for all of creation. You don't hold back the tender mercy that cost you so dearly, and I won't hold back from telling nations what you have done.

Your beauty and awe-inspiring majesty deserve the greatest of honors. You are the Creator who fills the earth with glory. Oceans thunder and fields echo ecstatic praise. It's time for the world to do the same. May thirsty souls be satisfied in your presence, as they come to know this One whose brilliance illuminates the sky.

Tear the veils from blinded eyes, so all will know your greatness that is beyond description. When the multitude of the earth surrenders pride and runs to you dressed in dirty garments and carrying heavy burdens, we will welcome them with open arms. Teach me to love them well.

The Voyage

Here's what I've learned through it all:
Don't give up; don't be impatient;
be entwined as one with the Lord.
Be brave, courageous, and never lose hope.
Yes, keep on waiting—for he will never disappoint you!

Psalm 27:14

Life with you is like a grand voyage! At times it is smooth and the way is clear. At other times, I am beaten by its raging seas. Through it all, you are with me, teaching me to walk upon the waters of adversity.

I've learned a lot on this journey—so much to discover in the posture of prayer. When I can't seem to find my way and I'm groping in darkness, you shine the light of deliverance and teach me of your faithfulness. When laughter overflows my soul, you are the source of joy. In answered prayer or seasons of delay, you are with me—watching and cheering me on.

You've taught me not to give up when my faith is tested and to cut off impatience like a flesh-eating disease. You've schooled me in the ways of courage and filled my heart with praise. You are the God of more than enough—the beauty of creation; heaven and earth's holy King.

The Lie

All this you have done and I kept silent,
so you thought that I was just like you, sanctioning evil.
Psalm 50:21

Lord, I long to eat from the Tree of Life. For too long I indulged in things that contained no nourishment. Following the paths that others coaxed me down only led me away from you. I hid behind a mask of holiness, but my heart was far from you. I lived to please others, instead of you. I was guilty of religion's greatest evil. Forgive me for sinning against you. I believed a lie.

Thank you for your conviction, which fell upon my heart. In your rich mercy, you revealed the truth that set me free. May I never live like a Pharisee again. I would rather have depth of spirit than to stand tall and proud for all the world to see. The applause of others is nothing, if I have lost sight of you.

Purify my motives, continually. Keep me free from a people-pleasing spirit. I want to carry the sound of love, so I will never be confused with the noise of a clanging symbol. I devote myself to you—to live for you and no one else.

Broken

Lord, bend down to listen to my prayer.
For I'm in deep trouble. I'm so broken and humbled,
and I desperately need your help.

Psalm 86:1

Lord, I'm broken. Life has beat me up, but I know you can put me back together. Though it feels as if things are beyond repair, I look to you. Come to my rescue. Sew the torn pages of my heart with your love.

I release all of my pain to you. Take it away. I choose to trust you even when I don't understand. I know you are good and you will get me through this. Let me hear the sound of love. Infuse me with your glory.

Nothing else matters but finding you. My desire is to fully know the One who is the answer to my every cry. Your grace is a refreshing fountain that strengthens me over and over. Even in the hard times, I know your purposes for me will not be thwarted. Your mercy is endless. I'm moving forward with you and never looking back. Your wisdom will lead me and I will rise in your victory.

Free from Fear

Listen to my testimony:
I cried to God in my distress
and he answered me! He freed me
from all my fears!

Psalm 34:4

You did it, Lord! You have conquered fear and I will never be held in its clutches again. As long as I am with you, I can face anything. I am brave. I am an overcomer. Fear will no longer dictate my life. And even if I have to remind myself of these truths, every moment of every day, I will no longer allow myself to be its victim.

When I stand in the midst of the unknown, faith will be the posture of my heart, even if my legs are shaking. Step by step I will walk into a life of freedom and never look back. I will trust you and release my concerns into your hands. Instead of fearing the challenges, I will thank you for them—they remind me to continually look to you.

I choose a life of victory, where you have full control. I won't be afraid of the things I don't understand. You are here. You are faithful. I am free!

Lessons from Creation

Tremble, O earth,
for you are in the presence of the Lord,
the God of Jacob.

Psalm 114:7

There's something holy, fearful even, that happens when you come on the scene. The earth senses it even when humanity doesn't. It responds and yields to your majesty. Waiting in stillness, the land anticipates you, its sole desire. The wind reaches out to reveal your pathways, yet only nature seems to notice. Oceans echo your breath with their movement, while trees dance and birds reply. I wonder if it's the stillness and the way the earth keeps you as its prime focus, which keeps it so sensitive to you. Oh, that we would learn from your creation.

Lord, teach me to be still. Truly still in the depth of my soul. To hear your whisper and not ignore your gentle nudges as I go about my day. To feel you in the touch of a stranger and find you in laughter's pulse. To pay attention to the joy you've placed inside of me and embrace it as a child. For peace to rule in the midst of chaos—where answers flow, though no one else hears.

Save Me

*I will hide beneath the shadow of your embrace,
under the wings of your cherubim
until this terrible trouble is past.*

Psalm 57:1

All I want to do is close my eyes and hide in your embrace until this trouble passes. Come and wrap me in the wings of your cherubim until then. You are the mighty God, my Father, the One who has always rescued me before. My cries reach to the highest heaven. I need you now.

The enemy has surrounded me like a fierce lion, just waiting to tear me to shreds. Come and trample him. Light up the sky with your shining glory as you soar through the darkened clouds of the enemy's camp. Show the whole earth that you're coming to save me and we will exalt you together.

Though I'd rather stay here where I know I'm safe, I'll turn to see what you have done. You've always been gracious to me. Always taken constant care of me. When I find the courage to look, I'm surprised by what I find—the very trap the enemy set for me has sprung shut upon him instead. You have saved me.

Now I can breathe again. For you have quieted my heart.

The Safety of Your Presence

When we live our lives within the shadow of the God Most High,
our secret Hiding Place, we will always be shielded from harm!
How then could evil prevail against us, or disease infect us?

Psalm 91:9–10

Lord, shield me from harm day and night. Send your angels to keep me safe. No matter where I go or what I face, if they are with me, I know I will be rescued from every trap. Not even disease stands a chance. I soar through the night like an eagle over high cliffs, undaunted by the enemies below. Hold me tightly in your strong arms, where the fiercest powers of darkness cannot touch me.

I set all of my affection upon you, for you are the hope that holds me. You've placed me under the shadow of your great love and are enthroned upon my heart. At times, when my mind runs rampant with anxious thoughts, I will turn to the peacefulness of your presence. Bowed before your mercy seat, I can rest without fear, because you are my confidence.

You have chosen me and all of my delight is in you. As I drink deeply of your love, I enjoy the fullness of salvation—the place where spirit, soul, and body are sheltered by your presence.

I Look to You

I will give all my thanks to you, Lord,
for you make everything right in the end.
I will sing my highest praise to the God of the Highest Place!

Psalm 7:17

I am yours. With unyielding devotion, I choose to live a life of faith. Though the journey is often filled with obstacles, and at times the world feels like an unsolvable puzzle, I look to you. You are the hand that holds me; the One who leads me with truth.

I relinquish the right to understand the process. Instead of striving to do what only you can do, I will lift my hands and sing your highest praise. Lord, silence the doubts and fears with your love. I trust you.

By faith I receive the answers that I long for. I will not run ahead of you, nor will I falter behind. You are the Lord of my life. Your promises are never failing. You are not a mere mortal who says one thing and does another. Your love is true. In the end, I know you will make everything right. I will remain steadfast and rest in your faithfulness.

So Be It

Shout hallelujah to Yahweh!
May every one of his lovers hear my passionate praise to him,
even among the council of the holy ones!

Psalm 111:1

Lord, I don't strive to be like everyone else. I am not looking to please others or conform to religion's demands; neither am I trying to be controversial. My only desire is to stay close to you—so filled with your brilliant splendor that I release it everywhere I go. If that sets me apart, so be it. I only desire to be who you have created me to be. I will wear no mask of pretense. I will not be named among the Pharisees.

Your love is like a furnace of fiery passion. It ignites my heart with songs of praise. I know others hear me, but I cannot hold it in! Let my zeal for you burst from me in flammable sparks that set others on fire. How impassioned I am to see others changed by your life-giving touch.

I want to eat and drink of you and boldly step into all you have for me. I want to live in the reality of your beauty so completely, I am robed with its radiance. Oh, that others would see you when they look at me!

Release

You can pass through his open gates with the password of praise.
Come right into his presence with thanksgiving.
Come bring your thank-offering to him
and affectionately bless his beautiful name!

Psalm 100:4

These burdens that I carry are way too heavy for me, Lord. In despair, I call to you—I can't see the path before me because it is hidden from view. As I stand at the border of your habitation, you remind me that I wasn't created to handle the torment of worry. You created me to live in faith, fully trusting you in every situation, experiencing joy and freedom.

Whether it is out of sheer obedience, or great despair, I'm not sure, but I lay these anxieties, doubts, and fears down. I choose to release the reins of my life to you. Take control and steer me in the right direction.

With thanksgiving on my lips, I move closer to you. I choose to remember your faithfulness throughout my life. Praise begins to overflow from deep within, washing me from the residue of anxiety and ushering me before your throne. When my gaze is upon you, I forget what I was worried about. This is the place of joy!

Throughout the Earth

Listen one and all!
Both rich and poor together, all over the world—
everyone listen to what I have to say!
Psalm 49:1–2

Father, let my words be heard throughout the earth. From my deepest musings, let my message be clear. Fill my speech with wisdom and insight, so that both rich and poor may understand. When I speak of you, saturate me with your life, so it will overflow into every word. Through my song, untangle the riddles that have confused people for ages. By my music, unlock the hidden mysteries of your love.

I pray that those who hear these words of wisdom would esteem them greater than wealth. For eternal life is worth the price, which no ransom could pay. Neither abundant treasure nor the riches of kings could satisfy the cost of sin. You have deemed our redemption too precious for anyone on earth to pay with earthly wealth. With joy-filled speech, I'll tell the world what you've done—how your love satisfied our debt and set us free. Merciful God, your spotless bride we will be.

Your Word

By your decree everything stands at attention,
for all that you have made serves you.
Because your words are my deepest delight,
I didn't give up when all else was lost.

Psalm 119:91–92

Thank you for your Word. By your decree everything stands at attention. Creation sits firmly in place as a testimony of your power. All that you have made gladly serves you. I treasure the revelation that streams from your Word—it is my deepest delight. Its wisdom guides me through the harshest storms.

Lord, I'm yours and I live my life to honor you. Grace me with insight—I set my heart before you. Teach me the profound revelations that others shun. I will absorb your eye-opening truth and walk in the light of your ways. Your promises are both thrilling and sweet.

Your Word is fastened to eternity. It has kept me alive. It gives me endurance when I want to give up. I've discovered that there is nothing perfect in this imperfect world except your truth. I rejoice in the power of your Word. It is my source of freedom.

Depths

I stand silently to listen for the One I love,
waiting as long as it takes for the Lord to rescue me.
For God alone has become my Savior.

Psalm 62:1

Lord, in your presence is everything I need. It is here, in the stillness of waiting, where my patience grows and I learn to trust you like never before. Come, meet with me. My heart yearns to encounter the realm of eternity within you.

The day seems brighter when I sense your nearness. Though troubles multiply, I am safe within your holy chambers. My soul is at rest in your wrap-around presence and worry no longer paralyzes me. Though fear competes for my attention, it has no place in me, for I have found strength in the depths of your love, which you so graciously impart.

I will not be moved by those whose vicious aim is to knock me down, move me from this place of peace, and distract me. My faith in you is unshakeable, with your glory as my guard. You are my Savior; my life-giving strength. I will wait in silence for you; remain calm and peaceful, knowing you will never fail me.

To Reveal You

He reveals mighty power and marvels to his people
by handing them nations as a gift!
Psalm 111:6

What an honor it is to be your child. How astonishing it is when I catch glimpses of your glory. Fill me with revelation, so I may understand your delightful mysteries, for your miracles astound me. Everything that you do is done brilliantly. Your perfection is eternal.

When you called me and placed your Spirit within me, I was overcome with rapture. Now you've asked me to reveal this love to the nations and it feels like you've entrusted me with more than I can handle. I tremble before you in holy fear. Pour out your wisdom, so I will never lack your loving understanding. Reveal your grace, for I cannot do this alone.

I know you will keep every promise you've made. You are flawless, faithful, and fair. Your forever-love has paid the full ransom for your people and you've called them to your side. Color me with the diversity of your love, so I will be a true reflection of who you are.

The Many Ways You Love Me

Lord, as we worship you in your temple,
we recall over and over your kindness to us
and your unending love.

Psalm 48:9

As I worship you, I must recall the many ways you love me. I will fill my spirit, soul, and mind with celebrations of your kindness. And be thankful—ever thankful. You care for me more than the birds of the field. You clothe me with your beauty. Every breath I take is a gift from you. Your holy blood flows through my veins.

The whole earth is filled with your glory, yet you've chosen to place your Spirit within me. Every sinew, organ, and every cell were carefully woven by your tender hand. How loved I am by the very One who *is* love. How blessed I am by your kindness.

Each day I enjoy the beauty of your fellowship. In every sunrise, I feel the warmth of promise upon my skin. When I rest my head to sleep, you soothe me with your voice. In sorrow and in pain, you lift me up to see your face. When evil looms, you prepare a table before me and calm my deepest fear. In times of joy, you dance with me on mountaintops.

You are so good to me!

Unstoppable Praise

In mercy you have seen my troubles and you have cared for me;
even during this crisis in my soul I will be radiant with joy,
filled with praise for your love and mercy.

Psalm 31:7

Nothing will silence my praise! Though my soul is bowed down in sorrow, I lift my voice and sing. You are good. You are a covenant-keeping God who will not forsake his promises. Your love is eternal. Your mercy is never-ending. You will refresh me in your presence, as I turn my gaze to you.

Though I feel utterly alone, I know nothing can separate me from your love. You are here and you will never leave me. I choose to remember your goodness and be thankful for all you've done. Every thought that exalts itself against you, I will arrest and put to bay. I declare you Lord over my mind and I relinquish these cares to you.

I will praise my way to victory! You love me. This is what I will recall over and over again. Your love never fails. Your sacred heart has inflamed my being and caused these fears to flee.

Transformed

*They grow stronger and stronger with every step forward
until they find all their strength in you,
and the God of all gods will appear before them in Zion.*

Psalm 84:7

Every moment with you is a like a moment of truth. Each time I turn my heart to you, ponder your Word, or think about your holiness, I am changed. With each choice I make to walk in righteousness, I grow stronger. As I behold your face, I am transformed—taking steps that take me from glory to glory.

Regardless of what comes against me, you find a way to use it for my good. Even my light afflictions will result in eternal glory. Your power has no limits. It can be seen in the smallest atom or heard in the fiercest wind. I'm humbled by your greatness. Without you, I am nothing. With you, I live a life of continual triumph.

I resign myself to do your will. By your grace, I will never stop pursuing you. Your presence is the secret to everlasting strength.

July

Alive

In all of my affliction I find
great comfort in your promises,
for they have kept me alive!

Psalm 119:50

Life is beautiful with you by my side. Your tender love woos and instructs me—always leading me on paths of freedom. Your promises keep me alive—they are my passion and my delight. The days seem brighter when I feel you near. The night is alive with whispers of your love.

Speak to me. I want to hear you in the quiet depths of my soul, even when distractions rage around me. Your words are life. They flood my being like warm honey—I can literally feel you flowing through me. When you speak, I'm revived and set free. Worry and anxiety fall away like broken pieces of a cumbersome, restrictive shell.

In every season of the soul, you are there—teaching, loving, providing. May I live with an open heart, able to recognize you in each one. As I meditate on you, light seeps into every dark crevice, clearing away the tangled webs of deception, and filling me with joy. You are the Beautiful One who makes me come alive.

A Life of Honor

Help us to remember that our days are numbered,
and help us to interpret our lives correctly.
Set your wisdom deeply in our hearts
so that we may accept your correction.

Psalm 90:12

Lord, I want to live my life with integrity—honorable and above reproach. You are eternal, immortal, the one and only true God. It is a privilege to live before your holy presence. I know that all of my faults and flaws are exposed by the radiance of your face. I won't run and I dare not cover myself with shadows to escape your eyes of fire that search my soul. There is nothing hidden that you don't see. Reveal anything that would separate me from you and I will embrace your correction.

Our life on earth is short. Each day, a precious gift from you. Help me to never take my existence for granted. I don't want to waste this treasured time and then simply pass away with nothing to show for it. Fill me with a heart of wisdom, so my life will count. May my works endure, simply because they have your breath upon them. As I walk in the splendor of your sweet beauty, may I leave behind a legacy of a passion, inspiration, and faith, for generations to come.

Glorious God

Sing and celebrate! Sing some more, celebrate some more!
Sing your highest song of praise to our King!

Psalm 47:6

God we love to celebrate you! You are awesome beyond words, the powerful King over all the earth. The world has never experienced a party like the one your loved ones have when we come together to praise you. With cheers, applause, and authentic adoration, we fill the earth with declarations of love and songs of thankfulness. What a beautiful sound!

You have always known what was best for us. You made sure our inheritance was taken care of before we even knew what an inheritance was. The way you honor those you love is mystifying. You conquered the nations and placed them before us, so we could rule alongside you.

Every noble and every prince will bow before you. Your throne has been established from the beginning of time. None could ever compare to you. Warriors lower their shields to honor you. Trophies are surrendered to your majesty—our triumphant King. We'll never stop singing. We'll never stop celebrating you, our glorious God!

Hiding Place

I trust you, Lord, to be my Hiding Place.

Psalm 31:1

Lord, sometimes I get stuck in the noisy distractions that play inside of my head. I despise these illusions, these traps set by the enemy to trick me into rejecting your truth. Don't leave me this way. Don't let me fall from this cliff and into the abyss of fear and torment. Grab me by the hand and pull me into the hiding place of your presence.

I close my eyes and take a breath, worshiping you, my only source of peace. I entrust my life to you—spirit, soul, and body. Guide me, deliver me, bring glory to your name. Though I'm exhausted, I will not turn away—I will trust in you and rest.

In the midst of crisis, I discover a well of joy bubbling within. The impossible becomes possible when you break open the way for me and paint it with beauty. How amazing you are! How faithful and true! You infuse these dry bones with strength, so they can dance again!

Ever Faithful

But the Lord says, "Now I will arise!
I will defend the poor,
those who were plundered, the oppressed,
and the needy who groan for help.
I will arise to rescue and protect them!"

Psalm 12:5

God, stand and defend the poor and needy. Expose the evil plans of oppressors and their lips will be silenced. As we cry and groan for help, rise in righteousness and rescue us from the wicked. You will never fail us!

We trust you—every promise you make, every word you speak is flawless in its very nature. The purity of your character sparks hope, igniting faith in your promises. You will forever keep us safe. You've proven over and over again that your commitment to us is true.

Ever faithful, you lift up those who are yours and keep us safe, while darkness prowls with pride in the shadows. With truth as pure as refined silver, you deliver the godly ones. You will not tolerate those who harass us. You are our Rescuer—the One whose arms keep us safe and sound.

Generous Living

Great blessing and wealth fills the house of the wise,
for they will walk in the way of the righteous.
Even if darkness overtakes them,
sunrise-brilliance will come bursting through
because they are gracious to others, so tender and true.

Psalm 112:3–4

You are the fountain of life that flows from my very depths. You have anointed me to minister hope to the hopeless and freedom to the captives. Though I may not know how to help everyone who comes across my path, you do. I will lean in to your Spirit and wait for you to speak. You will show me what to do and what to say. I won't ignore the hurting, nor will I turn a deaf ear to those in need.

Father, you have blessed me so abundantly. Now I want to be a living example of your love and compassion to others. I will not be selfish, but freely give, as I have freely received. Teach me to sow generously into the lives of those around me. Whether through time, finances, or simply a listening ear, help me to be an answer to the prayers of others. May my words be kind and my actions be sincere.

Everything I Need

O God of my life, I'm lovesick for you in this weary wilderness.
I thirst with the deepest longings to love you more
with cravings in my heart that can't be described.
Such yearning grips my soul for you, my God!

Psalm 63:1

Nothing and no one can satisfy the longings of my soul the way you do. Though this season has left me weary and worn, I reach for you more than any other. I don't care about anything else—I just need you. Refresh me.

I won't clamor to fight my way out of the dark cave, any longer. I won't curse this wilderness that has stripped me bare. Instead, I'll thank you for what you've taught me in the midst of it. You've taught me that your love is enough to get me through every situation. I've learned that when I lean back and rest in your arms, you carry me to safety. More than anything else, I've come to realize just how much I love you and how faithful you are—every time.

When I turn to you, every part of me is revived. Spirit, soul, and body, your presence fills every void. When I look in your eyes, your kindness restores me. Even though I've lost everything I once held dear, I am left with a foundation that can never be shaken. In you, I have everything I need.

More Than Enough

*I am passionately in love with God
because he listens to me.
He hears my prayers and answers them.*

Psalm 116:1

God, you are enough to get me through every situation. You listen when I pray and even when answers seem delayed, you always respond. As I walk through difficulties and hardships, you are with me. You wrap your love around me like a shield and strengthen me in the midst of battles.

It's so nice to know I always have your ear. You are the greatest listener. Even when I feel alone, you're here for me. Your presence chases away the heartache and fills me with joy. When I'm misunderstood and need your counsel, you wash away the sting of rejection, hold me close, and whisper words of wisdom. In the deepest darkness, you provide the light.

Your presence satisfies every part of me. Spirit, soul, and body, you fill each part. You replace sorrow with happiness and together we dance in the storms. You are the delight of my heart. Thank you for the way you care for me. You are more than enough.

Agape

He has conquered us with his great love
and his kindness has melted our hearts.

Psalm 117:2

You have conquered me with your great love. You are Yahweh, the only One who holds the power to melt the hardest of hearts. Just when I thought I understood love, I met you. You showed me what unselfish love looks like—pure agape, which flows effortlessly, expecting nothing in return. I'm so grateful; so zealous to love others the same way.

Lord, you have awakened me to experience the adventure of life with you. You have become my Beloved, my Forever Friend, and I am your bride. You held nothing back from me when you redeemed me with your love. In return, I will hold nothing back from you.

Take me over completely, so I will release the fragrance of your presence everywhere I go. Come closer—even to the places where I've tried to hide. You have set your love upon me and call me beautiful. I give all that I am to you, forever.

A Child of God

We can do nothing but leap for joy all day long;
for we know who you are and what you do,
and you've exalted us on high.

Psalm 89:16

Sometimes I can't help but shake my head in utter bewilderment that I am your child. Me—the child of God! With all of my faults and imperfections, fighting against the weakness of my flesh, yet called by your name and created in your image. It is absolutely astounding! You aren't embarrassed of me, you don't turn your head when I call, and you enjoy being around me.

All of heaven and earth bow before you. You are the Creator of all that is seen and unseen. Yahweh, the awesome Lord of Angel-Armies. Your throne rests on a foundation of righteousness, yet you've raised me up and seated me there with you. Mind-blowing!

When storms cause oceans to violate their boundaries, you command the waves and they obey. You're brilliant! Teach me to do the same—to be like you, my Father in heaven. Together we will walk side by side and release the days of heaven on earth. God, may I live forever in the radiance of your presence—the blissful place of life with you.

All-Consuming

God, our hearts spill over with praise to you!
We overflow with thanks, for your name is the "Near One."
Psalm 75:1

Lord, let me live my days sensing your nearness, as I do now. The very air I breathe is teaming with your life—it floods my veins and tickles my skin. I'm intoxicated by your love. Wave after wave of your affection floods my being, until I cannot contain my praise—it spills forth with untamed fervor.

The fury of love is all consuming. I don't know why anyone would want to resist. If they would only stand in the path of its intensity, they'd be swept up—never the same. Some boast that they have it all together, but I know that one brush with your love and their hearts would tremble.

Your presence—unpredictable and astounding—makes one weak and another powerful. It crashes against our chest like an avalanche of love. It knocks over the prideful, but causes the humble to increase in favor. Lord, all I want to do is lean in to its torrent and let it carry me where it desires. To resist is pointless. You have conquered my heart.

We Need You

Again I heard it clearly said,
"All the love you need is found in me!"
Psalm 62:11–12

Lord, I will trust in you and you alone. My soul is laid bare—I wear no mask to hide who I truly am. I pour out the longings of my heart and never pretend that I have it all together. There is no reason for anyone to profess to be something they're not.

We all need you. We strive and reach for so many things, but none quench the groaning of our thirsty souls. It is you we truly long for. The world, with all of its riches and trinkets, will never satisfy. Compared to you, it is all vanity—vanishing like vapors in a breeze. You aren't impressed with any of the ornaments we decorate our lives with. You look at our heart.

The power we seek, the strength we need, the joy we long for, and the love we admire—all come from you. For you are a flowing fountain of provision and grace. The greater our passion for more of you, the more you will give us.

Steady

I will never lose sight of your love for me.
Your faithfulness has steadied my steps.

Psalm 26:3

Lord, you know me better than anyone else does. You have searched my thoughts, examined every part of my life, and refined my heart. It is only by your mercy that I stand righteous. As long as I keep my eyes fixed on you, I will never stray.

I want the world to know I am intensely devoted to you, choosing to walk before you in honor. Your faithfulness steadies me. Your holiness reminds me that apart from you, I am nothing. I approach your throne with songs of thanksgiving, awed by the miraculous ways you've changed my life. I owe everything to you.

Look at what you've done for me—I'm not tempted by wickedness and have no desire to hang out with deceptive, conniving people. Establish me as one of your innocent ones, so I will never deviate from this remarkable path of faith. In your glorious presence, I have found my home. Thank you for your love.

To Be like You

May the words of my mouth, my meditation-thoughts,
and every movement of my heart be always pure and pleasing,
acceptable before your eyes,
my only Redeemer, my Protector-God.

Psalm 19:14

Father, you are the rarest of treasures—perfect in every way. Keep me close to your heart and speak words that cause my spirit to shine with your glory. Lead me, revive me, and fill me with wisdom.

How eloquently you declare your love for all of humankind. Through the beauty of your creation, you speak a language all can understand. The sun, moon, and stars all radiate with splendor, showing preference to none and grace to all.

Lord, help me to be like you. Teach me to walk in purity and correct me when I'm wrong. Draw me out of the shadows and into the light of your truth. There is nothing sweeter than the words of life that flow from your lips—the very words that said, "Light be!" and light was.

I pray that every thought I think, every word I speak, and every movement of my heart will always be pure and pleasing to you. Fill me with the power of your love that radiates through creation and resounds throughout my soul.

My Deliverer

Lord, I passionately love you!
I want to embrace you, for now you've become my Power!
Psalm 18:1

How deeply I love you, Lord. Nuzzled safe within your arms, I find strength to face any situation. You are the secret place to which I run and hide when I'm feeling overwhelmed. Nothing can touch me in the place of your towering protection. When it feels like the rug has been pulled out from under me, you are my firm foundation.

At times, when I'm too weak to move and all I can do is cry out to you, you come and rescue me. You throw the curtains of heaven open wide and ride the clouds just to get to me. Your love is astonishing! You come as a mighty storm, with breath of fire, to deliver me from chaos and calamity.

I feel you wrapping me in your presence, holding me tightly and overpowering my fear with your love. You illuminate my path with revelation light. All of a sudden I can see again! Beyond the darkness that tried to drown me, you have made a way for me. Empowered by your love, I have the victory.

My Friend

*There's a private place reserved for the lovers of God
where they sit near him and receive
the revelation-secrets of his promises.*

Psalm 25:14

I am your friend and I am always in your thoughts. You sit me beside you, in the place reserved for those you love. You whisper secrets that I alone can hear. You are pleased with me even when I disappoint myself. Your love is inexhaustible.

You never demand what I won't willingly give. You never push me to move in ways I don't want to go. You never force me to speak words that you long to share. You always take the humble posture of love, with no expectations. What a great Friend you are.

You are the Creator of the universe, yet you walk with me along the path of life and reveal truths that only you have known. You are great and glorious. Your promises cannot be revoked. How honored I am to have the beauty of your fellowship—the intimacy of friendship.

No Matter What

My soul, why would you be depressed?
Why would you sink into despair?
Just keep hoping and waiting on God, your Savior.
For no matter what, I will still sing with praise,
for living before his face is my saving grace!

Psalm 42:5

Lord, I have a lifelong account of your faithfulness. I shouldn't feel depressed when my faith is being tested, but this season of silence and waiting is wearing me down. You feel so far away. You've proven your love, repeatedly. You've answered my prayers many times before. Yet here I am, questioning whether or not you hear me.

Forgive me for sinking into despair. Reach out your hand and clear away the cobwebs of doubt and unbelief that have entangled my soul. Though you are quiet, I know that you're here—breathing hope and igniting faith that cannot be quenched.

I choose to focus on the things that are worthy of praise and will fasten my thoughts to the glory of your faithfulness. I will worship you through these dark clouds and believe you will pour out the harvest rains. Every place that the enemy has tried to defeat me will make me stronger. No matter what, I will not give up because you are good!

My Ultimate Quest

Make God the utmost delight and pleasure of your life,
and he will provide for you what you desire the most.
Give God the right to direct your life,
and as you trust him along the way
you'll find he pulled it off perfectly!

Psalm 37:4–5

God, I am consumed with longing to know you more. Penetrate my life with the substance of who you are. I want every passing image that runs through my mind, and the motivation behind all I do and say, to be pleasing to you. Grant me this request—to know you fully and to be yours unreservedly. I know that then every other part of my life will fall into place.

I release all other cravings to you. They are lesser loves that can never satisfy what my soul truly wants. No longer will I reach for ornaments of frivolous adornment, when I can be clothed with your beauty. I will hold nothing back from you.

You have captured me with the beauty of your ways and the power of your saving love. I've resigned myself to nothing less than unceasing communion with you. I will trust you unreservedly. Even when the path of life is surrounded by fears whose talons lash at my soul, I will be safe if I'm with you. I will fix my eyes on you and you will lead me on this beautiful adventure. You will pull it off perfectly!

Closer

I will come closer to your very altar
until I come before you, the God of my ecstatic joy!
I will praise you with the harp that plays in my heart,
to you, my God, my magnificent God!

Psalm 43:4

I wonder how close I may come and how much of your glory I can handle before I burst into a thousand flames. I am on a relentless pursuit. I want to know how much more there is for me to experience.

I know your love has torn the veil between us. I'm here with you, even now, but I want to come closer—every day. Over and over again. With words of adoration or in stillness of soul. And when I cannot contain myself, I will praise you with rapturous wonder!

You are magnificent—my ecstatic joy! You flood my senses with the substance of your love, until nothing else vies for my attention. Melodies of love rise from the depths of my being, like an instrument that only you can strum. No one holds my heart like you do.

In all of my yearning, I must remember you loved me first. You've shown me just how close we can be—you live inside of me.

Meet with Me

The God of passionate love will meet with me.
My God will empower me to rise in triumph over my foes.

Psalm 59:10

I'm bombarded by relentless storms; pelted by the rain. It seems just when the clouds begin to break, the showers fall again. The enemy seeks to wear me out and beat me down, but he will not succeed. I know in whom I believe. The foundation of my faith is found in you.

I lift my voice and sing your praise. You are faithful! You will not leave me this way. Your promises never fail. Goodness and mercy will follow me all the days of my life. These light afflictions are nothing compared to the glory that awaits me.

God of passionate love, come and meet with me. Speak the words of wisdom that will lead me into victory. Empower me to triumph over the wickedness that seeks to destroy me. I will not be defeated because I trust in you—the covenant-keeping God.

At Rest

God, listen to my prayer!
Don't hide your heart from me when I cry out to you!
Come close to me and give me your answer.
Here I am, moaning and restless.

Psalm 55:1–2

I'm listening, Lord. I feel you all around me, but I long for the certainty of your voice. Teach me to trust beyond the plans I make. Show me how to release my cares to you. Help me to live one day at a time, thankful for today's gift of grace.

I surrender my will to you. Forgive me for being restless and impatient. Though it feels as though you're hiding from me, I know you're near. You're ready to release perfect peace into my mind, as I fix it upon you.

The answers I need are hidden in your heart. All you ask is that I give you mine—without wavering in the face of fear. So I choose to do just that. I will drift upon the currents of your love, fully at rest and not needing to know where it leads. I trust you.

When My Heart Is Filled with Praise

Seeds of joy burst forth for the lovers of God!
So be glad and continue to give him thanks,
for God's holiness is seen in everything he does.
Psalm 97:11–12

Lord, everything you do is righteous and holy. Though I don't always understand the things that happen, my heart is set upon you. I will rest in the faithfulness of your ways. You know what's best for me. You will make a way.

When my mind overwhelms my heart and fights for the right to complain, I will bow before your throne of grace and yield my thoughts to you. Though tempted with confusion, I will choose to praise. I will commit myself to thankfulness and call to mind the many ways you've blessed me.

These unanswered questions will be satisfied by your love. The hopes that felt defeated, you will bring back to life. My spirit is empowered as I lean into your strength. Darkness doesn't stand a chance when my heart is filled with praise.

Embrace Me

So deep within me are these lovesick longings,
desires and daydreams of living in union with you.
When I'm near you my heart and my soul
will sing and worship with my joyful songs of you,
my true Source and Spring of life!

Psalm 84:2

Lord, come and meet with me. I know you're close, but you feel just out of reach. I long for your loving embrace. Breathe life into my spiritual senses, so every part of me is aware of you. Quiet the noise of the world and draw me into the stillness of your peace. Diffuse the fragrance of your presence, so I'm saturated with it. Let me taste the sweetness of your love.

Your presence is an experience both profound and satisfying, yet it stirs a hunger so deep I cannot get enough. I'm lovesick—needing you more than my daily bread. I don't want to love you from a distance. I want my heart to be a chapel of prayer—living in constant communion with you.

Flood me with streams of living water. May my life become a flowing, bubbling spring within me.

Listen

We are the lovers he cares for and he is the God we worship!
So drop everything else and listen to his voice!

Psalm 95:7

Lord, your voice is so sweet. I've heard it gently stirring within my soul, but I long to hear you more clearly. I yearn to know your voice so well that I never question what you say. When you whisper in my ear and tell me to go in a different direction, I want to be quick to obey. I'm leaning in Lord, speak to me.

Even more than that, I long for the sweetness and the power behind the sound. There's nothing I desire more than to be entwined with your Holy Spirit. As I live in unity with you, I will discover my true identity and flourish in all I do.

I earnestly desire the beauty of your fellowship in unbroken communion. Whether I experience you as a mighty rushing wind or simply have an inward sense of your presence, I trust you to reveal your love in the way that's best for me.

Tomorrow

You've gone into my future to prepare the way,
and in kindness you follow behind me
to spare me from the harm of my past.
With your hand of love upon my life,
you impart a Father's blessing to me.

Psalm 139:5

Lord, I release my future into your hands. Teach me to trust you in greater measure, where I'm not anxiously looking to tomorrow, but standing peacefully in today's grace.

You've already gone before me and declared that it's good. You are the provision for everything I need. I release my cares and the fear of the unknown, to you. I don't need to know what is coming, as long as your blessing is upon it. I will not dread what you have yet to reveal, because you've hidden it as a wonderful surprise.

My life is not my own. I've relinquished the right to control it. No longer will I concern myself with matters only you can handle. I give myself wholly to your will and choose to live in peace and faith-filled expectancy, fully trusting you. I will live in the glory of your presence and it will light the way. You have the power to make my dreams come true!

Victorious

> God's high and holy praises fill their mouths,
> for their shouted praises are their weapons of war!
>
> Psalm 149:6

Nothing will hinder my praise! There is no problem you cannot solve and no relationship you cannot heal. Despite the seeming contradictions that I face, I know you're with me. Your power is limitless. Your victory, guaranteed.

The same power that raised Jesus from the dead, lives in me. Nothing will stand in my way, if I only believe. Even when giants invade my Promised Land, praise is the weapon that will slay the biggest one. What a thrill it is to shout your praise and see walls of opposition fall!

This is what it feels like to be alive! You teach me to stand my ground while my cries of praise silence our enemies. You flood me with unstoppable joy as I extend my hands with shouts of thanks. This is the faith that overcomes!

What Do You See?

You, our Creator, formed the earth,
and you hold it all together so it will never fall apart.

Psalm 104:5

The world's beauty reflects you. If I look, truly look, I'll see you there. At daybreak, you announce your presence with light that pools through my window. Though I know it's the sun, I often wonder if the glory streaming from your garments is what illuminates the sky. Or perhaps it's your fiery passion for your bride that sets it ablaze.

As I step outside, the refreshing breeze brushes against my skin like feathers. I wonder if you fly upon the wings of the wind! From the nesting birds in the trees above, I hear the sweetest songs of love. Did they learn this lullaby from you? The fields are heavy with vegetables, grains, and fruit. You satisfy our hunger.

Everywhere I turn, I'm reminded of you. The thunderous skies, snow-capped mountains, the diversity of creatures, seas which support a vast new world—all of these, only a sample of the wild and wonderful world you've made.

You turn off the light and it becomes night. My head rests upon my pillow and I know I'm resting in your arms. You stretch out the sky like a glimmering tapestry, reminding me that even in the darkest times of life, there are always glimmers of hope, if we would only look.

Forever Grateful

What harm could a man bring to me?
With God on my side I will not be afraid of what comes.
The roaring praises of God fill my heart,
and I will always triumph as I trust his promises.

Psalm 56:4

My heart is overflowing, roaring with praise because of what you've done! I'm so grateful, Lord. I laid my fears before you, choosing to trust you, and you faithfully answered. You stored my tears in a bottle and kissed my cheeks. You've turned the tide and reminded me that mere mortals can do nothing to me when you're on my side.

Thank you! When I needed the help of a Father, you came running. Now I know I can trust in you fully. Your Word is true—never failing. Not a day goes by that someone doesn't harass me, but I'm not afraid anymore. Instead, I remain steadfast, praising you through it all. You have saved my feet from stumbling into the pit of death.

You bathe me in your life-giving light and show me the way to walk. The journey with you is filled with promise. You've proven your great love and I will be forever grateful.

My Resting Place

He offers a resting place for me in his luxurious love.
His tracks take me to an oasis of peace, the quiet brook of bliss.

Psalm 23:2

Father, I'm overcome by the glory of your presence. It is a spring of life, a bountiful brook flowing gracefully over my soul. The fragrance of your love is intoxicating, freeing me from all inhibitions. In complete surrender, I lean back and rest safely in your arms.

Pour the oil of your Holy Spirit upon my heart and massage it until all of the kinks have been worked out. Transform me. Lead me into the highest heights of your glory. Let my unhindered trust bring you the greatest honor.

In this place of peace, the pathway of your pleasure is easy to see. I can run through the darkness with you by my side. Fear cannot conquer me, because I know your love is unfailing and your goodness unmatched. You are my Shepherd, the One who fiercely protects me.

You have ravished me with your love and I am forever yours.

It Is Finished

His generation yet to be born will glorify him.
And they will all declare: "It is finished!"
Psalm 22:31

From time to time I have to remind myself that I can find you simply by praising you. But I have to be honest, it's not always easy. There are occasions when I struggle to see past the pain; beyond the evil swirling around me.

Yet with the simplest shift of my attention, I discover you are here—ready to prove how much you delight in me. You've never left me; you'll never forsake me. Since the moment I was conceived, you've cradled me with love. How easily I forget, how hastily I abandon my courage.

Regardless of my propensity to be led by my mind, instead of my heart, the truth is indisputable—you are holy. You are enthroned within the praises of your people. Your faithfulness has endured for generations and you have delivered me many times before.

Though no one else can help me, you can, and you are more than enough. I cannot take credit for anything—the very love I love you with is a gift you've given me. You are the reason for my praise. I will stand in boldness and declare, "It is finished."

You Are My Heart's Desire

Lord, because of your strength the king is strong.
Look how he rejoices in you! ...
For you have given him his heart's desire,
anything and everything he asks for.
You haven't withheld a thing from your betrothed one.

Psalm 21:1–2

Blissful. I endlessly partake of this love that knows no bounds. Lord, the radiance of your face is like a wildfire of love. Your holy passion blazes through my veins with unquenchable fire. The flames of affection are unstoppable, consuming those who stand against you.

Every encounter with you is filled with blessing. As I adore you, you place a royal crown upon my head and clothe me with garments of glory. I can only bask in your splendor and lift my hands to honor your majesty. I am astounded by your love. I discover anything and everything I could ever want, living within you.

It is only by your strength that I can stand in your presence. You are the king of my heart—ruling with passion that is stronger than death. I've tasted of your love, now help me to never turn away; to never forget that it is by your grace alone that these blessings flow. Your eternal love holds me tightly and never lets me go. You are my heart's desire.

August

Break Open the Way

I cried out to ... the delivering God. ...
Suddenly the brilliance of his presence broke through
with lightning bolts and with a mighty storm from heaven—
like a tempest dropping coals of fire.

Psalm 18:6, 12

Lord, I love you. You are powerful and strong, shaking the whole earth with one glance of your eye, yet with gentle whispers you soothe my soul. Fire encircles you and flames leap forth from your mouth, but I'm safe, hidden within the armor of your love.

You're dressed in garments of mystery, soar with the wings of spirit-wind, and with a mighty roar you part the seas, revealing the depths beneath. Yet, when I cry you hear. When I feel myself sinking beneath the weight of adversity, you reach down from heaven and deliver me.

You are my secure foundation. You reward me with your blessing because I have kept my heart upright before you. Fill me with your strength as I worship you with simple abandon. Let your love break open the way for me, leading me beyond all fear and into victory.

Though you are majestic—and your power incomprehensible—you surprise me with kisses of truth, for I am fully yours.

Hope

I'm consumed with longings for your promises,
so I ask, "When will they all come true?"
Psalm 119:82

I'm lovesick, consumed with longing to see your words come to pass. I've known your love in the hardest of times—wooing me closer and restoring me. Even when my soul felt dry and shriveled, I knew you were there. Now I know, in these seasons of waiting that you are here. Your truth is eternal. Never failing.

I will stay steadfast, never yielding to thoughts of despair. Though your promises delay, I trust you. Revive me with your love and spare my life with your kindness. You are my living hope; faith's foundation. I will be content in the valleys and shout on the mountaintops—you are good.

When darkness screams and hope fades, you roar with truth. You are the fire of certainty that cannot be ignored. I will rest in the fury of your love and receive your peace that passes all understanding. You will not forget me.

Chosen

Lord, you have chosen Zion as your dwelling place,
for your pleasure is fulfilled in making it your home.
I hear you say, "I will make this place my eternal dwelling,
for I have loved and desired it as my very own!"

Psalm 132:13–14

You have made your home in me. Joy floods my being as I ponder the reality of your mercy and grace. I am amazed that you would consider me. The greatest of fables could never compare. Yet this is real—Almighty God choosing to dwell within me.

Increase my faith in this paradox—the merging of omnipotent God with feeble man. My existence is the very manifestation of your love. I am your chosen one. I want to honor you by living in the reality of this wondrous truth and demonstrating it to the world around me.

Your glistening glory rests upon me like a robe of righteousness. You've placed a crown upon my head that sparkles with jewels of salvation's power. Holiness blooms within me. My life flows with milk and honey. I will worship you forever.

Unity

This heavenly harmony can be compared to the dew
dripping down from the skies upon Mount Hermon,
refreshing the mountain slopes of Israel.
For from this realm of sweet harmony
God will release his eternal blessing, the promise of life forever!

Psalm 133:3

Father, release the power of your glory upon the earth. Let true harmony flow between believers, so we'll be examples of compassion for all the world to see. How truly wonderful, delightful, and beautiful it is in your sight. In this place of sweet unity, pour out your blessing.

Breathe faith into us again and teach us of ways much higher than we've known. Let your power flow through us as we become an extension of your love. As your glory is seen upon us, let it be anchored by humility, integrity, and love. May we be a reflection of your goodness. May we learn to honor, support, and celebrate each other. May we comfort the hurting and strengthen the weak.

Release the light of your truth to those who walk in darkness. Finish the work you have begun and manifest your character within us as we love with unconditional love.

Wonderful

Shout hallelujah and praise the greatness of God! ...
All you worshiping priests on duty in the temple,
Praise him, for he is beautiful!
Sing loving praises to his lovely name.

Psalm 135:1–3

The atmosphere changes when you walk into the room. Though we cannot see you with our eyes, our spirit knows when you're near. You surround me with your love and my heart is set on fire with blazing flames of holy passion. As I lift my hands in worship, I feel the breath of life—your Spirit abiding within.

Your presence stirs me to praise. You're the reason I sing; the treasure I have sought. How beautiful you are! Even your name is lovely.

Day and night I ponder your wisdom. There is no limit to your power and authority. You extend your greatness throughout the entire universe. Miracles are seen throughout the land. From misty clouds you bring wind and rain; the sky thunders at your command. No other god can compare. Jehovah, you are wonderful and your name endures forever!

Captivated

Every single moment you are thinking of me!
How precious and wonderful to consider
that you cherish me constantly in your every thought!
O God, your desires toward me are more
than the grains of sand on every shore!
When I awake each morning, you're still thinking of me.

Psalm 139:17–18

The way you love me is astounding. Yours is a profound love that has always been and always will be. You know every detail of my life. You understand me in ways I don't yet understand myself. You cheer me on when others stop believing in me. Before my day begins, you go before me to prepare the way.

I want my heart and soul to flow in unison with your Spirit—a most graceful *pas de deux*. Come, inspect the hidden places of my being with your searching gaze. Examine me and reveal anything that would lead me down an evil or painful path. I will not pull back from your cleansing fire.

I want to know you the way you know me. I want to see you clearly. You have ruined me for anything other than the glory of your love. Nothing else matters. I am captivated by you. Yet I know you love me more. If I were to count your thoughts for me, they would be more than the grains of sand upon all the shores.

Outrageous Love

Escort me along the way; take me by the hand and teach me.
For you are the God of my increasing salvation;
I have wrapped my heart into yours!

Psalm 25:5

God, my heart is yours. Every day with you is a new adventure. All that I am—spirit, soul, and body—is yours. I hold nothing back. I run into your arms, knowing you love me simply because you do. You've even taken the time to number every hair on my head.

My heart is full—flowing like a river and saturated with your life-giving splendor. Every day I want to soak in your glory—from the moment I wake through the dark of night. Teach me to wait upon you with expectancy. Speak to me and wrap me in the power of your beautiful words.

Give me glimpses into the vastness of who you are. I want to discover things about you that you've hidden up until now. I love when you come—when you pour your grace upon me and pull me into your embrace. Your love for me is outrageous. I never want to leave.

Fearless

In the depths of my heart I truly know
that you have become my Shield;
You take me and surround me with yourself.
Your glory covers me continually. You alone restore my courage;
for you lift high my head when I bow low in shame.

Psalm 3:3

Lord, cover me in your glory and unchain me from the yoke of fear. Restore my confidence and make me brave. I wasn't created to live in the torment of dread. You've called me to be fearless.

Fear has been destroyed by the expanse of your power. I will not be dominated by unruly imaginations that contradict your truth. Facts will not faze me, because your Word is never failing. Ignite faith within me as I submit my thoughts to you. I'll shake off the doubt and stir myself to praise.

When I feel you with me, I can conquer any mountain. Your voice alone sparks courage. My heart comes alive when you speak. I will stand and face my enemies and look fear in the face, with you as my shield. Hope rises when I remember— you believe in me.

Desert Garden

In the days of desert dryness [God] split open the mighty rock,
and the waters flowed like a river before their very eyes.
He gave them all they wanted to drink from his living springs.

Psalm 78:15–16

Thank you for the wilderness seasons of my soul. As I look back, I realize those were the seasons I saw your greatest miracles. In the driest, most painful times, your love was the most profound. The lessons I learned about your faithfulness in the midst of devastation have become precious treasure to me.

It was then that you enclosed me in the fragrant garden of your love and taught me how to find you in ways I never had before. I discovered how zealously you pursue my heart. I learned that your presence would soothe the pain of a soul bowed low. You taught me the value of surrender and how beautiful my songs of abandon could be.

You became more real to me than any other time. Your love became the fountain I drank from day after day. Darkness became my friend because it taught me how strong I could be when I depend on you.

Lord, though these times are never easy and often confusing, thank you for what you do through them.

Lead Me

Lord, even when your path takes me through
the valley of deepest darkness,
fear will never conquer me, for you already have!
You remain close to me and lead me through it all the way.
Your authority is my strength and my peace.
The comfort of your love takes away my fear.
I'll never be lonely, for you are near.

Psalm 23:4

The longer I walk with you, the longer I trust the paths you lead me on. Even when it seems that you're leading me in circles, you're actually leading me higher into the purposes you have for me. Fear no longer has a place in my heart, because you have become the King who rules in the midst of it.

I am confident when you take me by the hand, even when I don't know where we're going. In a thousand different ways, you prove your goodness and love for me. Your authority gives me peace.

I am never alone. You're always right beside me and even when I cannot see you, I know you've got my back. Through the lowest valleys or over mountain peaks, I live in the light of your presence. Doubt is no longer an option. I trust you.

Higher

Look how you've made all your lovers to flourish like palm trees,
each one growing in victory, standing with strength! ...
Listen to them! With pleasure they still proclaim:
"You're so good! You're my beautiful Strength!
You've never made a mistake with me!"

Psalm 92:12, 15

Sometimes I don't understand why you do the things you do. Your ways are so much higher than mine. You open doors I don't feel ready to go through. You give me dominion over an earth I don't feel qualified to steward and tell me to rule and reign. It's more than I can fathom.

Yet here I am, holding the keys to the kingdom of heaven; called to rise and shine. I know you never make mistakes and that you define me by who you are in me, but at times I feel hesitant. Hold my hand, so I won't stumble and fall. Help me to remember the greatness of the One who lives inside of me.

Each day I will come before you and listen for your instructions. I will release the atmosphere of heaven within me as you lead me to the people who need your love. You will never ask me to do something I'm not anointed to do. From glory to glory, you will take me. You are my beautiful Strength.

Good Morning, Lord!

At each and every sunrise you will hear my voice
as I prepare my sacrifice of prayer to you.
Every morning I lay out the pieces of my life on the altar
and wait for your fire to fall upon my heart.

Psalm 5:3

Morning shines forth with radiant splendor. I bow in worship and wait for your fire to fall upon my heart, sparking flames of holy adoration. The way you welcome me into your presence leaves me awestruck. You always make me feel at home, even though you are the Righteous King.

My passionate prayer rises before you and I find myself wrapped in your love, covered by a blanket of mercy. A canopy of kindness and joy overshadows me. Your commitment to me is extravagant in every way.

I can't contain my excitement as each day I walk beside you, knowing you're leading me in the direction that's best for me—the perfect path, one filled with promise. Lord, you deserve my highest praise. Your faithfulness causes me to burst forth with joy; I sing as loudly as I can!

The way you bless the righteous amazes me. Those who are so wonderfully blessed will declare your faithfulness forever. As we reach out to you, you bring us the victory; in the end everything will be set right.

You Haven't Forgotten Me

You will answer me, God;
I know you always will,
like you always do as you listen
with love to my every prayer.

Psalm 17:6

God, I have to admit, sometimes it feels as though my prayers have fallen on deaf ears. I listen for you, but it seems you're so far away. I feel alone, as if I'm hanging on for an answer to my prayers that may not come.

With anticipation I wait. I turn to you and will not relent.

My tears write the story of my pain and with tender loving care you read each one. You take your time and search my heart. You haven't forgotten me. I remind myself that this fiery trial is nothing compared to the flames of your passionate love.

I choose to trust in you, laying aside my questions and complaints. Everything within me knows the truth: you are the faithful one, my Hero who always comes to my rescue. Merciful and gentle, your kindness never fails.

You answer my prayers in ways I couldn't have imagined. Father, my heart is filled with joy and peace because of who you are and the way you love me. Thank you for coming.

Praise!

Listen everyone! Sing out your praises
to the God who lives and rules within Zion!
Tell the world about all the miracles he has done!

Psalm 9:11

When you walk into the room, I explode with praise! You're the merciful King who has come from his throne to answer my prayers and fill me with hope. When the enemy rises against me, just one blast of your thunderous judgment causes him to run and hide. Humbled, I stand in your holy presence, wanting nothing more than to honor you.

How righteously you rule. You're merciful; the Lord of all eternity who lives and reigns forever. I cannot stay silent. I must tell the world of your faithfulness—the way you rise to help those in need and work wonders that are nothing short of miraculous. You will never reject us; never disregard our cries for help.

My heart is bursting with joy! I knew I could count on you, but you have exceeded my expectations. You brought me out of the pit of despair and all I want to do is celebrate. I'll sing and dance and shout your praise. The Lord of eternity, our mighty God, lives and reigns forever!

Rise

All rise! For God now takes his place as Judge of all the earth!
Don't you know that everything and everyone belongs to him?
The nations will be sifted in his hands!

Psalm 82:8

Father, you are the voice of true justice. Rise and let the courtroom of heaven convene. Speak and declare your judgments upon those who have judged on your behalf, revealing their errors. Teach your representatives how to discern between right and wrong—lead them by example. Shake the weak foundations of our society to the core and expose corruption. Deliver our leaders from darkness and ignorance. As the Most High, set the standard for integrity and lawfulness.

Everyone on earth belongs to you—from the poor and seemingly forgotten, to the rich and powerful. None are hidden from your sight. Help us to be just like you, with hearts of compassion and lips dripping with wisdom. Enlighten our society with joy and thanksgiving. May respect and morality be the norm. Let a spirit of unity run freely in our streets as you become the motivation for every deed and the center of every soul. We look to you.

Awakened

Awake, O my soul, with the music of [God's] splendor.
Arise my soul and sing his praises!
I will awaken the dawn with my worship,
greeting the daybreak with my songs of light!

Psalm 108:2

I greet the morning with melodies that stream from my heart. Within my soul, songs of love are awakened. Faithfully you greet me each day, diffusing the sweet fragrance of your presence and drawing me out. Your love is extravagant, reaching higher than the heavens.

Lord, I want to soar with you over mountains peaks and watch as you pour out your glory upon the earth. As you speak from your sanctuary, I will be listening—leaning in to catch every whisper. The words that flow from your heart are like a kiss upon my life, equipping me for battles we will face together.

My song rises to you with passionate praise. Your atoning love has triumphed over anything I may face. Today, wherever I go, I will keep my mind set upon you—you are the strength of my life. My song of joy ... forever.

Called to Shine

The heavens belong to our God; they are his alone,
but he has given us the earth and put us in charge.

Psalm 115:16

What an honor it is to glorify your name. To be known as a passionate lover of God. To know the very One who formed me, the Creator of heaven and earth. I trust more in your love than in my ability to accomplish great things. You've placed the earth in my charge—stay close to me. Unlock the fears that hold me back. If I shine, it is only because you are shining through me.

As I bow in reverence before you, you give me more. More of you. More peace. More joy. Most of all you satisfy my soul, yet you flood me with unquenchable desire to know you even more. Blessings upon blessings overflow in my life and will continue through the generations.

Your promises are my delight. With humility I listen as you speak within my heart. Lead me beyond the borders I have set for my faith. Help me to remember who I am—the me I don't yet see.

Faithful

Keep on giving your thanks to God, for he is so good! ...
Let all his lovers who bow low before him sing:
"His constant, tender love lasts forever!"

Psalm 118:1, 4

Your constant, tender love lasts forever! That's the theme of my heart. For so long I felt stuck—it seemed the wilderness season would last forever. My leaders could only help me so much, but the breakthrough I needed could only come from you. Sleepless nights offered me the chance to continuously turn my heart to you. Though my faith was sometimes weak, I knew it would be better to trust you to save me than to put my confidence in the frailty of human flesh.

Now I will live in my divine destiny! I knew you wouldn't forget me and you didn't. You delivered me into a beautiful broad place! You showed me the pathway to your presence and I never strayed. I rushed through your gates with praise that defied every enemy standing in my way. I lifted my hands in surrender and offered you songs of love regardless of how I felt.

But I take no credit—not even for my love. Even that is a gift from you. I survive because of your grace. So I will declare, over and over again—you are good! Your constant, tender love lasts forever!

Through It All

All you lovers of God who want to please him,
come and listen, and I'll tell you what he did for me.

Psalm 66:16

Lord, I'm exploding with excitement over what you've done for me. You brought me through the fire and purified my heart. I won't lie, it wasn't easy. At times I felt like a prisoner who couldn't break free from bondage, but you were with me through it all. You never gave up on me. You visited me with words that freely flowed into my heart, massaging out all of the kinks. Those living words washed over my soul until I could see clearly again. I wouldn't have made it without you.

You saturated me with your goodness and gave me rest. It was then I realized that my own sin was keeping me from you. If I would have closed my eyes and ignored your correction, who knows where I'd be now. Instead, your grace drew me in. You never ignored me, never cast me aside, not even at my darkest point. You loved me through it all—saw the best in me, even when I couldn't see it in myself.

I finally realized that in all of my reaching, in all of my striving, it was you I was longing for. Now I will live for you, holding nothing back. Let the fragrance of my life ascend as sweet-smelling worship to your heart.

Your Glorious Dwelling

Zion-Mountain looms in the farthest reaches of the north,
the city of our incomparable King!
This is his divine abode, an impenetrable citadel,
for he is known to dwell in the highest place.

Psalm 48:2–3

God, you never cease to amaze me! I thought I knew so much about you, but then you introduced me to your holy city. There are so many reasons to praise you and now I've discovered more. How beautiful your city is! How majestic the mountain upon which it sits. You dwell within its highest heights. Those who live with you are safe and sound within this impenetrable citadel.

Your home is more splendid than the grandest of castles. This divine abode is glorious—the kings and queens on earth would be jealous. It's hard to believe this is where I will get to spend eternity. Perpetually filled with joy, living a life of victory, and celebrating your unending love and kindness—it's almost too wonderful to imagine. All who come here will sing and dance with never-ending praise.

Instead of waiting, I'll live a life of heaven on earth, right now! I will rejoice and echo your fame all around the world. Everyone will know how much you love us and of this beautiful place you've prepared for those who love you.

My Bridegroom-King

Now listen, daughter, pay attention,
and forget about your past. ...
For your Royal Bridegroom is ravished
by your beautiful brightness.
Bow in reverence before him, for he is your Lord!
Psalm 45:10–11

I bow in reverence before you, my Lord. My heart is on fire. I feel your eyes upon me—your bride to be. You tell me that I'm beautiful and glorious, as I appear before you in your holy chamber. Though I do not feel worthy of such affection, I gratefully and humbly accept—it is only because of your suffering love that I stand before you now. I am not defined by my past. With all of the confusion it brings, I gladly leave it behind.

As I stand beside you, I'm overcome by heaven's fragrance surrounding us. The crown of bliss is upon your head. The oil of joy drips from your fingertips—I've never seen anyone as happy as I see you now. I feel the same way—glistening in the glow of your pure golden glory. You are handsome and wonderful. I'm bursting with excitement over who you've called me to be.

I come before you ready to pen our sacred story with the beautiful lyrics that stream from my grateful heart. I will make sure that everyone remembers what you've done for me. I honor you, my Bridegroom. You are the King of my heart.

Living Waters

My soul thirsts, pants, and longs for the Living God.
I want to come and see the face of God.

Psalm 42:2

God, I'm thirsty; consumed with thirst that only you can quench. I long to drink deeply from the refreshing waters that flow from your presence. My soul is parched, desperate for your living waters. I must see your face. Only then will I be satisfied.

I'm heartbroken. My pillow is wet against my face—drenched with tears that will not relent. So I speak to my heart, *Take courage!* Find strength in the joyous praise you once knew. Remember his faithfulness. Refuse to be depressed. Keep hoping. Keep waiting. Stay steadfast, and no matter what, never stop worshiping and praising him.

I turn my face to you, my Savior. I seek the light that streams from your face like the morning sun blazes against the mountainside. You bloom through my dreams with whispers of love that awaken my heart. Ever true, you pour out a deluge of passion that cascades over my soul and sets me free. I drink freely of the abundance of your love once again.

You Alone

Now, God, I'm left with one conclusion.
My only hope is to hope in you alone!

Psalm 39:7

Lord, the countless expressions of your love far exceed my expectations. Forgive me for the times I've doubted. For the times I've allowed the cares of this world to cloud my vision and choke my faith. Life is too short to spend my time striving to make everything perfect.

You alone are my only hope. I've finally realized that everything I am and all I have comes from you. And without you, life itself is irrelevant—a fleeting shadow lacking substance.

Even when I doubt, even when my tears are the only words I have, your merciful love breaks through the lies and breathes truth into my spirit. A new song rises within me and hope replaces anguish. This is why I love you! You always find a way to encourage me. You never leave me to wallow in the sludge of self-pity. You lift me up, and with a smile that could illuminate the darkest of nights, you celebrate what I'm yet to become.

My Beautiful Inheritance

Make God the utmost delight and pleasure of your life,
and he will provide for you what you desire the most. ...
Quiet your heart in his presence and pray;
keep hope alive as you long for God to come through for you.

Psalm 37:4, 7

Lord, in you I'm totally fulfilled. The longings of my heart are satisfied as I feast upon your faithfulness. Hope comes alive when I'm in your presence. My sense of security cannot be bought. All the money in the world could not purchase what I have—the blueprints to an abundant existence.

With faith that pleases you and captures your attention, I give you full control. I release the reins of my life into your hands. As long as I trust in you and fix my heart upon your love, I know you'll take care of the rest. So I quiet my heart in your presence and hope in you continually.

You're the fulfillment of my dreams, my beautiful inheritance, the foundation upon which my world stands. You'll never leave me or forsake me. Instead, you love me.

Deeper

I am standing in absolute stillness, silent before the One I love,
waiting as long as it takes for him to rescue me.
Only God is my Savior, and he will not fail me.

Psalm 62:5

God, pull me like a magnet into your presence. Let me sink deeper and deeper into your love, past every distraction. You are the core of who I am; the center of all I do and think. You have unlocked my heart and poured in your Spirit. Such a beautiful mystery—you in me and I in you.

At times I can do nothing more than wait on you in absolute stillness. I may not hear your voice or feel you near, but you give me a sense of peace that all is well. Even when you seem far away, it is my delight to lavish you with my songs of love and whispers of adoration. You are worthy of my affection—always.

Oh, but then there are the times when your tangible glory touches my skin, hovering so close that I wonder if I can finally touch you. Your beautiful love floods my senses, making me fully aware that you are here. You never forsake me. Without fail, you always come.

Safe

You will be guarded by God himself.
You will be safe when you leave your home
and safely you will return.
He will protect you now,
and he'll protect you forevermore!

Psalm 121:8

Day or night, no matter where I go, I know you are with me, keeping me safe. Your presence wraps me like a shield of protection. Your angels have set up camp all around—they watch out for me and keep me from getting hurt. When I sleep, I can rest in total peace, knowing that wherever I am is a zone of safety. Even my dreams are blessed.

I lift up my family and friends to you as well. Go before them and make every crooked path straight. Guard them from sickness, harm, and tragedy. As they go about their days, be the armor that covers them continually and bless them with long and beautiful lives.

Guide me through times of adversity with wisdom and a clear head. Even when I walk into situations that are filled with evil and darkness, I know that the Light of the World lives inside of me—I will not fear. I will walk right through the midst of it releasing your presence. Thank you for being my continual Hiding Place, my Shelter from harm!

Content

Lord, my heart is meek before you
I don't consider myself better than others.
I'm content to not pursue matters that are over my head—
such as your complex mysteries and wonders—
that I'm not yet ready to understand.

Psalm 131:1

Thank you for this amazing life you've given me. Although it is filled with ups and downs, you are teaching me the joy of contentment. I can savor each day, knowing we walk through it together. Peace fills my soul as I remember your goodness and focus on your love.

I'm so grateful for your blessings—both big and small. Everything you give me has been fashioned perfectly, just for me. May I never take your tender care for granted. Help me to never stress about what I don't have, when you've given me so much. There is always something to be thankful for.

I want to live in simplicity and peace, without striving to always have more. Teach me to rest and enjoy the many beautiful things around me—the elegance of a winter snowflake dancing to the ground, the fragrance of spring, summer's glorious sunset, or the way you paint the leaves in autumn. Tune my ear to hear the pleasure of a baby's laugh, or the voices of those I love.

This is how you intended life to be: content—simply living every day enjoying you.

My Healer

O Lord, my healing God,
I cried out for a miracle and you healed me!

Psalm 30:2

Your love is constant—never changing. Yesterday, today, and forever, you remain the same. The healing power that flowed from your hands so long ago still reaches to mend me now.

Sickness and disease must bow to your mighty power—the stripes of Calvary sealed the deal. Health and healing are mine—body, soul, and spirit. Flood every organ and cell, even the blood that flows through my veins, with your heavenly glory. Strengthen my bones, muscles, and ligaments, so I can finish this race in victory.

Lord, heal my mind so every thought lines up with yours. Let peace and joy rule over all other imaginations. Pour out your love, so fear cannot abide. I release unforgiveness and bitterness, so they will not poison my soul. Touch every fiber of my being, so I will enjoy the long and vibrant life you created me to have.

Continually

Everything I am will praise and bless the Lord!
O Lord, my God, your greatness takes my breath away,
overwhelming me by your majesty, beauty, and splendor!

Psalm 104:1

God, when I stand in your presence, I'm overcome. Your love pierces my heart and sets it ablaze with unquenchable zeal to know you more. My eyes are locked on yours—I cannot look away. I don't want to. Your beauty and splendor are matchless. You are holy and majestic. No one in heaven or earth compares to you. Let your love cascade upon my heart, until it feels like only you and I exist.

Don't let my own wandering thoughts pull me away from the awareness of you. I want to abide in a continual experience of your glory. Each day living in constant collisions of heavenly encounter. Words, hopes, dreams, and extensions of your love to others, overflowing from the core of who I am when I'm with you. I dedicate myself to a lifestyle of giving and receiving love.

Inexhaustible

We rebelled against God's Word ...
so he humbled us through our circumstances. ...
Then we cried out, "Lord, help us! Rescue us!" And he did!
Psalm 107:11–13

Lord, I'm in constant need of your help. No matter how many times I cry out for you, you always come. Thank you for being so gracious to me.

I know you love me and will never forsake me, but sometimes my flesh rises up and starts to doubt. Yet even when I'm sinking in a sea of confusion, you lift me up and encourage me with eyes that hold no condemnation. Your love is inexhaustible—it never runs dry.

You're so merciful and kind. I'm constantly pursued by your goodness and unfailing love. Fill me with hope as I remember your victory. Ignite my faith as I meditate upon your Word. Just as the birds of the air fly upon your breath, I too will rise above. Faithful Lord, you will never leave me and never tire of coming to my rescue. You're so good to me.

Promise

Just a little while longer and the ungodly will vanish;
you will look for them in vain.
But the humble of heart will inherit every promise
and enjoy abundant peace.

Psalm 37:10–11

Father, thank you for the many beautiful promises you've made me. I'm amazed by the power they hold. They aren't empty promises given to stir hope but then disappoint. Every word you speak is true and alive. You desire the best for me in every part of my life.

You came so I would have an abundant life. I will not wander around in doubt and unbelief. I will not retreat when things get hard. Though sometimes it seems like the manifestation of these promises are just out of reach, by faith I will grab them and pull them from heaven to earth. I will trust you and your timing, because I know how much you love me.

I commit every aspect of my life to you. Align my words and thoughts with your truth. You are my Deliverer, Provider, Healer, Savior, and Friend. Give me fresh perspective and wisdom for each facet of my life. Pour your blessings upon me as I seek your face. Guide me with your eye.

September

First Love

What joy overwhelms everyone who keeps the ways of God,
those who seek him as their heart's passion!

Psalm 119:2

You loved me before I ever knew you existed. You sacrificed yourself for me, revealed your love, and wooed me, all because you didn't want to be without me. When you opened my eyes, you became my first love. No one could ever compare. Now, with all of my heart, I devote myself to you.

My soul is overjoyed because of the miracle of this love. I come alive as I continue to seek you before everything else. My life is brighter and happier, all because I walk with you. Every day is filled with endless possibilities, when I put my priorities in order. Spirit, soul, and body—I am blessed in every way.

With so many things competing for my affection, give me grace to keep you first. Even in seasons of extreme busyness, may you always be my soul's delight and profound passion. Unite my thoughts to be one with yours. Help me to always respond to love's gentle pull and keep my heart from growing cold.

Simply Because I Love You

The life that pleases me is a life lived in the gratitude of grace,
always choosing to walk with me in what is right.
This is the sacrifice I desire from you!
If you do this, more of my salvation will unfold for you!

Psalm 50:23

Lord, thank you that you don't give me a to-do list. With all of the demands placed on me by others, it's nice to know your love is unmerited. My lifestyle of devotion flows effortlessly because of the posture of my heart—it allows me to find you in every moment. There's nothing I can do to make you love me more than you do right now. I do what is right, simply because I love you.

Getting to know you is so enjoyable! Sitting quietly in nature, resting in the stillness of worship, laughing with friends in joy-filled conversation, talking about you, even thinking about you—all become acts of worship when my heart is fully yours. These also become ways that you speak and reach out to me. I'm beginning to notice you in every setting.

Loving you isn't something I can check off my to-do list. It's a beautiful, enjoyable journey of discovery filled with peace and joy, not stress. It's a part of who I am. I'm so thankful for your grace.

Strengthen Me

Lord, in my place of weakness and need, I ask again:
Will you come and help me?
I know I'm always in your thoughts.
You are my true Savior and Hero,
so don't delay to deliver me now for you are my God.

Psalm 40:17

God, I need your grace for today. Strengthen me. Refresh me. Revive me. I'm tired, weary, and want to climb under the covers and stay there. I know you're here with me now. I turn my heart toward you. Just a moment in your glory begins to rejuvenate me.

You are so kind. When I have days of not feeling well physically or mentally, you always offer your tender love. You pull me aside to rest when I need it. You breathe hope and joy into my soul. When I dread what the day may hold, you remind me that your grace is more than enough to sustain me. You push fear away by wrapping me in your love.

I lean into your presence, close my eyes and breathe you in. I hear the songs of love you sing over me. Even now, my body is receiving health and stamina. My mind is becoming focused, clear, and hopeful. There is no mountain I cannot climb, no obstacle I cannot leap over, when you hold my hand and lead me in with grace.

In Love

My praises will fill the heavens forever,
fulfilling my vow to make every day a love gift to you!
Psalm 61:8

Your presence is like a beautiful, fragrant garden. It soothes me. It causes me to stop what I'm doing and take notice. It draws me in, just to enjoy its splendor. Hold my hand. Let us sit together in the stillness of this most glorious place and exchange our gifts of love.

Your love blossoms within my soul, stirring cravings for more. What a delight you are! You are a faithful Companion, a most trustworthy Friend, and a magnificent Savior. The radiance of your smile chases away the darkest of days.

What joy I've found in your presence! What sweet release! There's a sparkle in my eyes and a skip in my step—the sure sign of a person in love. Oh, that you would smother me over and over again with your holy kisses.

Victory

My God, I will sing you a brand-new song
when you give me the victory!
The harp inside my heart will make music to you!

Psalm 144:9

You created me to live in victory! When trials come, no longer will I look at them as setbacks, or let it ruin my day. I will keep my focus on your goodness, your love for me, and the promises you've made me. Seasons of hardship will be viewed as opportunities to offer you heartfelt trust and faith-filled praise. These times are nothing more than opportunities for my next victory.

I was created to be like you, Jesus. I will walk on the waters that try to drown me. Peace will be such a perfect friend that I'll sleep through the rockiest of storms. You will strengthen me with your joy.

I choose to step into the victory you already bought for me. My declarations of faith will unlock the treasures of heaven and move the tallest of mountains. Even in the midst of the fire your love will sustain me, because I am your child. When I feel weak, I will lean into you and you will perfect your strength within me. I am an overcomer—nothing will keep me down.

Father

You own the day and the night.
Sunlight and starlight call you Creator.
The four corners of the earth were formed by your hands,
and every changing season owes its beauty to you.

Psalm 74:16–17

The sun and the moon call you Creator, but only I can call you Father. You have fashioned the entire world from the beauty that resides inside you, but only I was made in your image. Creation, in all of its splendor, takes my breath away, but only I move your heart.

Hidden within nature are secrets of your love. The cooling wind is like your refreshing breath. You raised the brilliant sun to give light to the whole earth, just as your Son is the light of the world. Rainbows of promise, oceans that thunder your voice, and trees that wave their arms in praise—all point to your creative genius.

You are seen in all you have made. But only I am called your masterpiece—a humble vessel of divine majesty. What an honor it is to be a child of the King!

Lift Me

I am burdened and broken by this pain.
When your miracle rescue comes to me,
it will lift me to the highest place.

Psalm 69:29

Lord, rescue me! My heart is heavy and my head is spinning. I wasn't made to lie down in defeat, I was created for victory. Hide me in the cleft of your rock, before the ground cracks open and swallows me up.

I draw the line at my sanity—the enemy will come no further! I refuse to be sucked into a pity party. I don't live in discouragement or despair, because I live *in you*. You are good. Your miracles never cease. You love me.

Tear down the doors to my past. I don't want to look over my shoulder at what once was—whether painful memories or longings of nostalgia. You are my present reality and my hope for the future. I leave it all behind to walk with you.

I give you permission to move my heart—always toward you, in constant streams of devotion. Don't let me go my own way. Lift me into the highest realms of your glory. Never let my love run dry.

Begin Again

Revive us again, O God! I know you will!
Give us a fresh start!
Then all your people will taste
your joy and gladness.

Psalm 85:6

Sometimes it's easier to imagine my fears than to see with the eyes of faith. I know it shouldn't be, but too often it's true. I need a fresh start. Come and revive me; be my song of victory again.

You are powerful enough to rule the world, yet gentle enough to calm my heart. When I'm weak and weary and cannot hear your voice, you restore me in your love. Though at times it feels as though you've stripped me bare, I will bloom again in a barren land. I will find joy in the midst of the fire because you are here.

Mend this broken and bleeding heart. I was created for joy and destined for greatness. Sorrow will not hold me earthbound. Teach me to fly with these wings you've given me, so I will soar over the mountains with you.

From Beginning to End

Magnify the marvels of your mercy to all who seek you.
Make your Pure One wonderful to me,
like you do for all those who turn aside
to hide themselves in you.

Psalm 17:7

Lord, you are the foundation of my devotion. The bedrock upon which I build my life. Help me live my life in the divine order of your glorious kingdom. I want to live in the light of your truth, with no compromise to divide my soul.

Each morning I start my day with you. I will give you my first and best. I know everything flows from the place of your presence and without you, I would painfully strive in all I do. Nothing is more important than you. You are my first love. I will have no other loves before you. I want my life to be an altar of perpetual consecration and to love you with all of my heart, mind, and strength.

I hide my heart within your reality. I delight in your Word. Empower me with your grace, so I will never follow after other gods—the love of money, the pursuit of worldly lusts, or idols of pride—let them never be said of me. When things go well, help me remember your faithfulness.

May my life honor you until the end, so I will finish well.

Aware

*You have captured our attention
and the eyes of all look to you.
You give what they hunger for at just the right time!*

Psalm 145:15

You captivate me, Lord. I think about you all of the time. How beautiful you are! How kind. I'm alive because of you. Each beat of my heart is because of your faithfulness toward me. Every breath I breathe is a movement of worship. I never want a moment to pass by where I've forgotten you. I want the posture of my heart to always be toward you—aware of your love.

I feel the presence of heaven—brushing against my skin and filling my lungs. It is overtaking every other thought. Your nearness sparks hope and gives me eyes to see the paths that once were veiled. When I'm with you, I am filled with wisdom. Suddenly, things that seemed impossible become goals worth pursuing.

You never stop changing me—I'm constantly going from glory to glory and from one glorious revelation to the next. You know exactly what I need at precisely the correct moment. You won't open doors I'm not ready to go through and you will not barricade the way that fulfills my dreams. What I hunger for, you satisfy with your love.

I Shall Not Want

My heart, O God, is quiet and confident all because of you.
Now I can sing my song with passionate praises!
Psalm 108:1

There's nothing like resting in the stillness of your love. Your presence quiets the noise in my head and the chaos all around. Each moment I'm in your arms, rivers of peace cascade over my soul. I'm so grateful for this love.

A continual conversation stirs deep inside. God and humanity living in unhindered communion. This is where it all begins—where passionate prayers fall like jewels from my lips. Even when I'm overcome with wonder and cannot utter a word, my soul swells with never-ending melody.

Your presence is intoxicating—imparting confidence beyond my understanding. When darkness overshadows me, you shine your light of love, so I can see clearly again. It is then that I discover that everything I desire is found in you. I shall not want for any good thing when I am consumed by this love.

God of Peace

The Lord alone is our radiant hope
and we trust in him with all our hearts.
His wrap-around presence will strengthen us.

Psalm 33:20

Nothing can separate me from your love. Regardless of how I feel, you are here with me. I am forever cocooned within the shelter of your presence. You will strengthen me with your joy as I hide myself in you.

You alone are my radiant hope. When gray clouds obscure my view, you are the reason I sing. My praise ignites a spark of light that becomes an unquenchable fire within me. Discouragement doesn't stand a chance.

Whether abounding in joy or suffering loss, I know in whom I believe. I will bravely bear my cross and walk by faith, trusting what I cannot see. In you I am courageous. Your nearness empowers me to roar with holy passion and believe in who you've called me to be. Your love conquers my doubts and fears. I will trust in you. You are the God of peace.

You Are Good

Hallelujah! Praise the Lord!
It's time to sing to God a brand-new song
so that all his holy people will then hear how wonderful he is!
May Israel be enthused with joy all because of him,
and may the sons of Zion pour out
their joyful praises to their King.

Psalm 149:1–2

God, you are the joy of my heart, the celebration of my soul! I will shout it from the rooftops—you are good! You are the victory that overcame the grave. You are the reason I sing and the passion that stirs me to dance.

When my affections are set upon you, nothing seems impossible. I see you in every situation. Even in the darkness, because I know you are the answer. You are the fiery breath of breakthrough who fills my life with glory.

What a glorious honor it is to live in your presence. While I sleep, my heart is awake, streaming with melodies too marvelous for words. By day, I lift my hands in holy surrender; my heart is open to you. Praise rises from within, in uncontrolled waves of laughter—the crescendo of blissful love. Yes, you are very good!

A Cry for the Lost

The Lord builds up Jerusalem;
he gathers up the outcasts and brings them home!
He heals the wounds of every shattered heart.

Psalm 147:2–3

God, gather the outcasts and bring them home. So many have lost their way, led astray by the schemes of the enemy; restore them to us. Run to them with your mercy. Leap over the walls they have placed in front of you and conquer them with your love. Make yourself undeniably real, once again. I stand before you on their behalf.

The spiritually homeless have nowhere else to turn. Their faith has been crushed to dust. They grasp for answers that can only be found in you, yet they are blinded by confusion and pain. Breathe life into their dry bones, heal the wounds of their shattered hearts. Release them from their self-made prisons. Transform them with your love.

You are the victory that brings the dead back to life—the beauty that will soon be seen upon them. Illuminate their darkness with the glory of your love. They will become nothing more than blood-washed fragments of who they have been. I praise you, for the battle has already been won! Your love is stronger than death!

Worthy of My Praise

Hallelujah! Praise the Lord!
My innermost being will praise you, Lord!
I will spend my life praising you and
singing high praises to you, my God, every day of my life!

Psalm 146:1–2

Hallelujah! God, I will praise you forever! You have become the theme of my heart, overflowing in unceasing melodies. Creator of heaven and earth, there is no denying your might. You dismantled the power of darkness within me. Now I'm alive within the mystery of eternity.

Your love has no beginning and no end. Through it you turned the sacrifice of death into a victory vast enough to save the entire world. No one can compare. Neither noble leaders, nor the world's most brilliant minds were the ones who established heaven's glory—you alone did that with perfected wisdom.

You are the splendor that shines in the midst of obscurity; whose touch brings me strength. Hope comes alive as I praise your name. Faith finds its home as I lean into your words. Because of you, my heart is filled with joy. You are worthy of my praise!

Come

Let the dawning day bring me revelation
of your tender, unfailing love.
Give me light for my path and teach me, for I trust in you!

Psalm 143:8

Lord you are faithful—you've always been and you always will be. Come as you have so many times before and save me by your gracious Spirit. For you are true to your promises and by keeping them you are glorified even more.

O righteous God, have mercy on me. Spare me from your judgment and answer me with your loving kindness. When my heart is heavy and dazed with despair, I remind myself of the glorious miracles you've already done. Though it feels as if my life has been crushed to dust, I know you'll answer me.

I thirst for you like the dry cracked ground thirsts for rain. I reach out to the only One who can save me. You are all I need. Illuminate my soul like the dawning day. Come quickly and fulfill your word. I wait for your deliverance.

The Fragrant Offering of My Life

Guide me away from temptation and doing evil.
Save me from sinful habits and from keeping company
with those who are experts in evil.
Help me not to share in their sin in any way!

Psalm 141:4

God, pour out your grace upon me. I want my life to be a pleasing offering—a fragrant incense rising before you. Guide me away from temptation and reveal hidden sin that would disconnect me from your ways. Drench me in your tangible goodness, so I cannot be lured by sin's invitation.

When others correct me, I will receive it like healing medicine and choose the path of the humble. I will not be offended, even if they're wrong. In this place of vulnerability, I invite you to reveal truth that sets me free.

You have called me your own. Help me to keep my heart, mind, and soul flowing in complete harmony with your Spirit. Teach me the ways of honor and integrity. Make my life a fruitful garden that feeds the hungry soul. Purify the motives of my heart. Wash me in your cleansing love.

Not Forsaken

O Lord, you are my God and my saving strength!
My Hero-God, you wrap yourself around me to protect me.
For I'm surrounded by your presence in my day of battle.
Lord Yahweh, hear my cry.
May my voice move your heart to show me mercy.

Psalm 140:6–7

Lord, I'm surrounded by evil on every side. The enemy wants nothing more than to destroy me. Life seems like a constant fight between fear and trust. My mind is constantly trying to rationalize this attack that has left me weary. I wish I didn't feel this way, but I do.

Though this wilderness has become a prison, I know you're by my side. You will rescue me and set me free. You are my God and my saving strength. Even in this battle, when at times I'm only vaguely aware of your presence, I choose to cherish your nearness more than anything else. I lay reasoning aside and trust in you.

May my voice move your heart. May this glimmer of hope within me become a majestic mountain of faith. Let your love quell the raging fears. You are here with me, walking through the darkest season of my life. You will not forsake me.

Children of the Kingdom

Children are God's love-gift;
they are heaven's generous reward.

Psalm 127:3

Lord, bless the children. Let them know you as Father, Friend, and Savior. Make yourself real to them, so they will never stray from your great love. Give them wisdom and understanding to follow your Word. Clear the paths for them to walk on. May your love be their sure foundation. Grant them peace and protect them from harm.

Guide them by your Spirit. May others know them by their integrity and compassion. Strengthen them in dark times and teach them of your faithfulness. May they understand their worth and flee from youthful lusts. Unlock their identities as they find themselves in you.

Be their treasure. Fill their lives with joy as they dance upon foundations of praise. Be their grace and inspire them to greatness. Acquaint them with your love that never ends.

Invincible

Those who trust in the Lord are as unshakeable,
as unmovable, as Mighty Mount Zion!

Psalm 125:1

Unshakeable. Unmovable. Bolder than a lion. That's how I feel when I'm surrounded by your presence. Without you, everything seems to be an insurmountable task. With you, I'm invincible!

God, you're the answer to every problem. You are health and peace, prosperity and wisdom, joy and forgiveness. You extinguish my fears with the fury of your love. You are the strength of my life. Help me to quiet my mind, in order to hear you clearly. Your voice will shift the destinies of cities, regions, and countries.

Your goodness is a gift of unmatched value. The triumph of your love, more powerful than death. It gives me courage to stand when everything around me is shaking. Together we can conquer every difficulty, for with you nothing is impossible!

Jerusalem

Pray and seek for Jerusalem's peace,
for all who love her will prosper!

Psalm 122:6

I pray for the peace of Jerusalem. May her cities be filled with praise. May the prophecies spoken over her come to pass. Surround Jerusalem with your protection. Dwell in her midst as you woo her with your love.

Lord, be glorified within her gates. Shower the land with your blessing, so the people—your people—will taste of your goodness. May she be an example of your faithfulness and power, so the nations will see you in all your glory. Bring peace to her borders. Restore her.

You are the covenant-keeping, miracle-working God. Open the eyes of their understanding, so all may see you and know you as their Savior. Be with them in trouble, cover them, and deliver them. They will be your people and you will be their God.

Protected

Jehovah himself will watch over you;
he's always at your side to shelter you safely in his presence.

Psalm 121:5

I have built my life upon your love. Creator of heaven and earth, you are always by my side, sheltering me and protecting me. When the storms of life rage, you are the foundation that cannot be shaken.

So many times I have looked for help that is tangible—something I can grasp with my hands and see with my eyes. But then I realize that you are my true help. You're never too busy for me. Day or night, you are with me—always watching over me, even when I don't realize it.

You alone are worthy of every song, of every breath, of all of my praise. You declared peace over me. You redeemed me from every curse of destruction. The atmosphere changes when you are near, and I know you'll keep me safe. I rest under the shadow of your wings. I delight in your love.

Reveal Your Justice

Lord, listen to my heart's cry,
for I know your love is so real for me;
breathe life into me again by the revelation of your justice.

Psalm 119:149

I lie awake pondering your promises. I've wrapped your words into my life—they've become a part of me. I remind myself you are for me. You are with me. Now I'm asking you to answer my passionate prayer.

Reveal your justice in my life. Defend me. I'm crying out for mercy. Breathe life back into me again. Let this desert become a fruitful garden. Redeem me and revive me, just as you said you would. I long for your salvation.

The injustices I've suffered tried to suffocate my faith and failed, but I'm weak—dependent upon your strength. Be the center of every conscious thought, the peace of unconscious musing. I know your truth is powerful and unchanging—reveal it to me afresh. Establish me in your love and give me courage to dream again.

Discover

*I was desperate for you to help me in my struggles,
and you did!*

Psalm 120:1

You are the source of my joy. Your presence is indescribable. As you lead me beyond my temporary struggles, I find that life with you is a journey of discovery. I can find you anywhere, if only I would look.

With you, life is beautiful. You ignite my heart with blazing flames of holy passion, so I'm consumed with thoughts of only you. This is the place of freedom. Suddenly my vision is clear—the paths that once were hidden come in to view. You are there, beckoning me forward and inspiring me toward greatness.

In this place of holy love, the veil of separation no longer exists. I have you with no distance between us. Fear is nowhere to be found. Wisdom's voice leads me from day to day. Peace becomes my best friend. Heaven is open over me.

Knowing You

Let my prayer be as the evening sacrifice
that burns like fragrant incense, rising as my offering to you
as I lift up my hands in surrendered worship!

Psalm 141:2

Lord, I delight in you. May my life be as a fragrant offering. I am here—with you now and every moment. I worship you upon an altar of pure devotion. I hold nothing back. All I desire is to be close to you and to have more of your presence in my life.

Your breath fills my lungs and I exhale with cries of love. I want you to hear my songs of adoration—to see the words rising from my heart and filling the air around me. I'm burning with unquenchable fire—the passion to come even closer. To be consumed by your perfection and purity.

You are in me, around me. And I am in you. I lift my hands within the atmosphere of your glory. Descend upon me in all of your goodness. I want to smell like you and release the bouquet of your beautiful perfume everywhere I go. I let go of every distraction and invest myself fully to this one pursuit—knowing you.

I Am Loved

It's impossible to disappear from you
or to ask the darkness to hide me;
for your presence is everywhere bringing light into my night!

Psalm 139:11

There's no escaping your presence. It's impossible to flee from your searching gaze. You see it all. You know my coming and going before I even take a step. You're already in my future and were with me in the past. You're my present reality—with me at all times.

Goodness and mercy follow me everywhere I go. Even in my most miserable moments, when all I want to do is run and hide, you explode through the darkness and illuminate my path. You never leave me. You're waiting for me at every turn.

Every aspect of my life is precious to you. You're the keeper of my dreams, both great and small. There isn't one fleeting hope that escapes your eye. Rich in mercy, not even the stain of sin would make you hide your face. How beautifully you love me!

Indescribable

Serve and worship the awe-inspiring God.
Recognize his greatness and bow before him,
trembling with reverence in his presence.

Psalm 2:11

God, you're amazing! You know the stars by name and breathe light into the moon. You are wisdom's origin and love's true substance. Every hope that fills my heart and each mountain of faith I climb are all because of you. You're the beauty I discover in every brilliant sunrise; the wonder I experience when I listen to ocean waves. You're my delight—the joy that brings me to tears and evokes laughter so deep it makes no sound.

Omniscient God, I'm overwhelmed by the glory you pour into this vessel of flesh and bones. What a wonder and delight you have chosen me, when all I have to give is myself. At times your holiness is more than I can bear.

I'm undone. Completely and utterly undone by this love. It's indescribable—more profound than any words I could write or sing, much deeper than any movement of dance, stillness, or painter's brush. You fill the earth with splendor, yet your arms were stretched wide for me.

The Posture of Love

You've kept track of all my wandering and my weeping.
You've stored my many tears in your bottle—not one will be lost.
You care about me every time I've cried.
For it is all recorded in your book of remembrance.

Psalm 56:8

You are a perfect Father and a true Friend. Over and over again I come to you crying out for help, and you never refuse me. I've lost count how many times I've fallen heartsick at your feet, but you haven't. You hear every prayer I pray and care enough to write them all down.

You always take the humble posture of love—ready to listen and eager to give. No matter where I go, you're with me. You counsel me with perfect wisdom and strengthen me with redeeming grace. My burdens never turn you away. My weaknesses never disappoint you. Every tear is precious to you.

I will rise and bring you endless glory. Thank you for your patience and for loving me so completely. Though I've wandered, searching to discover where I belong, I finally realized your presence is a perfect home.

Firmly Planted

We will not fear even when the earth quakes and shakes,
moving mountains and casting them into the sea!
For the raging roar of stormy winds and crashing waves
cannot erode our faith in you.

Psalm 46:2–3

I've planted my feet firmly within the soil of your love. Though trials come, trying to choke my faith, I know in whom I believe. You, my God, are faithful—a covenant-keeping God who cannot lie.

When the crashing waves of adversity pound upon my mind, I will yield my thoughts to you. I want to be so fully at rest and hidden within your love that I can sleep through any storm. Lift me above the waters and shield me from the howling winds.

I will not allow the darkness to have a place in my soul. Fear is but an illusion that I cannot afford to partake of. Wrap me in your light, so I can see things from your perspective. Refresh me. My faith in you will stand, because I am rooted and grounded in eternity. Diffuse the fragrance of your peace all around me as I release my soul to you.

Perfected Beauty

God's glory-light shines out of the Zion-realm
with the radiance of perfect beauty.

Psalm 50:2

Lord, you are the perfection of beauty. Your glory is infinite, blazing from your fiery heart. When I encounter your presence, I'm astounded; wondering if I can endure it, yet I long for more. I want to see you without restraint; every part of me experiencing the totality of your holiness.

You are the very origin of love's pure light. Rise upon your people and beautify us with yourself, so our lives stream forth in radiant splendor. Manifest your grace and kindness through us. As true worship rises from our midst, let our passion be contagious—seen in all we do.

I love you. You are my joy and my delight. Your beauty inspires me. I want to touch it—this brilliance that lights up the sky and illuminates the darkest of hearts. I want to know you as I know my closest friend. Perfect me in your love and never let me go.

October

Still My Trembling Heart

*In the day that I'm afraid, I lay all my fears before you
and trust in you with all my heart.*

Psalm 56:3

God, you're so close, but I need you to come closer. Fear is screaming in my face and I'm afraid. Silence these lies with your truth. My mind has drawn a blank—the only thing I know to do is to run to you. I believe. Help my unbelief.

Still this trembling heart. Touch my eyes, so I can see through the thick fog of doubt. I lay before you, surrendering my brokenness. Bind my bones with words of strength. Hold me within the shelter of your love, so it will be well with my soul once again.

Breakthrough is coming. I hear it—like the sound of many waters cascading over the mountaintops. I must not give up. Though hope is but a smoldering ember, the fuel of love will ignite it afresh. My weakened faith is strong enough to carry me to you.

Continual Delight

Keep me in this glory.
Let me live continually under your splendor-shadow,
hiding my life in you forever.

Psalm 61:4

Your glory is astounding—I never want to leave. Your love has collided with my darkness, transforming me day by day. Come, sit with me. Speak to me. I want to know you more and to live in this place of undistracted devotion.

In you I come alive. Your love has set me free. Let me abide here for all eternity—under the shadow of your wings; safe within your arms. I am yours forever. Having tasted the pure and undefiled delicacies of your house, I am ruined for anything else. You are my continual delight.

My greatest desire is to be found in you—embraced so fully by you that I'm unrecognizable. I want to hide my life in you. In you—where I live and move and have my being. In you, where I discover my true identity. Longing for you is a beautiful gift.

Extravagant Love

Your love is so extravagant it reaches to the heavens!
Your faithfulness so astonishing it stretches to the sky!
Psalm 57:10

I'm here, in the intoxicating delight of your gentle yet immediate nearness. Your love has come—permeating every part of me, leaving nothing untouched by the radiance of your glory. I'm undone! I never want to withdraw from this place of rapturous bliss.

The price of love that once flowed from a wooden cross now rests upon this heart of flesh. A love so vast that earth alone cannot contain it. An ever-springing fountain that satisfies the greatest thirst. Be exalted as you soar throughout the heavens, your shining glory on display.

Oh, to know you as you know me! To see clearly those eyes that blaze with fire! To hear the voice that crashes upon the waves. Your love is extravagant. It reaches to the heavens and extends throughout the earth. When I lay my head upon your chest, I hear nations calling and I remember—love is meant to be shared.

Vessel of Honor

Here's my life motto, the truth I live by:
I will guard my ways for all my days.
I will speak only what is right, guarding what I speak.

Psalm 39:1

I choose to be a vessel of honor. To guard my words and fill my thoughts with holy meditation. Lord, it's so easy to voice what I feel and yield to the pressures that try to defile me, but that's not what I want to do. I want to live in purity and surround myself with people of like passions.

You're my reason for living. You're worthy and beautiful. You're wisdom and creativity, peace and joy. I want to please you with a life of purpose and humility. Teach me to listen to what flows from my lips, so I will know what is in my heart. Help me not to grumble and complain, but to be thankful in every situation. Allow me to see the shadows that try to obscure my iniquity.

From now, throughout eternity, I desire to live before your glorious light. I lift my hands in full surrender. Touch my lips, Lord, so they will only speak what is holy and true. Cleanse my heart, so it beats in tune with you.

Delight

The steps of the God-pursuing ones
follow firmly in the footsteps of the Lord.
And God delights in every step they take to follow him.

Psalm 37:23

I want to be known as a lover of God. As one who passionately pursues you with unrelenting devotion. Live inside of me in all of your wonder. Draw me into a lifestyle of holy zeal as I follow in your footsteps. Never let me be named among the Pharisees, who wear masks of religious piety, stemming from the desire to please people.

At times we have rested beside still waters. At other times you have taught me to skip among the mountaintops. But now I want to run with you. To share this story of love that you have written upon my heart. To hold your hand as it reaches with love for others. To speak as you speak and give as you give. I want to witness entire nations turning to you in a day.

With no other motivation than to love well, I pray my heart would be pleasing to you. As I trust in you, seeking to do what's right in your eyes, I will fix my heart on your promises. My eyes are set upon you. I'm secure in you, and you're my delight.

Confidence

*Hide all your beloved ones
in the sheltered, secret place before your face.
Overshadow them by your glory-presence.
Keep them from these accusations, the brutal insults of evil men.
Tuck them safely away in the tabernacle where you dwell.*

Psalm 31:20

Darkness cannot overcome me, for you have made me yours. I'm called by your name, filled with your Spirit, covered in grace, and surrounded by favor. In my weakness, you make me strong. In times of sorrow, you bring me delicacies of delight.

You alone are the Faithful One! Day by day, as I seek your face, you tuck me away in the shelter of your love. There I will remain—overshadowed by your glory, hidden from the enemy.

Every pit that was dug for my destruction, becomes a mountain of praise for me to stand upon. Trials become something to be thankful for, because I know that they are my future strength. When others walk away, you give me grace to draw near.

Fear is swallowed by your victory. You have become my confidence.

God of Miracles

You have kept me from being conquered by my enemy;
you broke open the way to bring me to freedom,
into a beautiful, broad place.

Psalm 31:8

You did it, God! Just when I thought you'd forgotten, you broke open the way and set me in a beautiful, broad place. Now I stand on the side of answered prayer, with arms lifted high and heart filled with praise!

God of miracles, nothing is too hard for you. I had become a shell of what I once was—tortured by a season of pain and delusion. No matter how hard I tried, nothing changed. But then you came! Now I am stronger than before. My trials became a launching pad, catapulting me into the greatest freedom I've ever known. My tears of misery have become tears of joy and thankfulness!

Now I see how faithful you are. My entire life, my every moment, my destiny—it's all in your hands. You love me. You have a purpose for my life, and though at times I can't imagine how it will come to pass, you know it all. You will not forsake me.

I'm so happy! I can't thank you enough. You're the God of miracles!

You Are the One

This is the One who gives his strength and might to his people.
This is the Lord giving us his kiss of peace.
Psalm 29:11

Carry me to your house; to the very chambers of your love. Kiss me with peace and let the winds of your Spirit strengthen my soul. For you are the only one who can love with both tenderness and power.

Your voice topples the strongest of enemies, yet it soothes the surrendered soul. It ignites flames of undeniable love to those who listen and empowers us for victory. Your touch awakens the slumbering heart. Your love is the breath of life. You're here. And you're everything I need. All I can do in the beauty of this moment is worship you.

Your love rises within me—undeniably real and overwhelmingly powerful. Flow through my veins, infuse every cell, and illuminate every thought with the glory of your presence. Over and over again, flood my life and never stop. Let the evidence of your palpable existence pour out of me everywhere I go. I never want to be without you.

Loving Myself

You love me so much and you placed your greatness upon me.
You rescued me from the deepest place of darkness,
and you have delivered me from a certain death.

Psalm 86:13

When I think about your love for me and how the Creator of the universe has chosen to live inside of me, I can't help but say, "I must be amazing!" Lord, teach me to walk out this revelation in both humility and joy. Help me to love and believe in myself, the way you do.

You have destined me not only for greatness, but to find happiness—just by being me. You placed a part of your character inside of me, which only I can display. It makes me unique. I am a child of God and you know me by name. I must be pretty special. Help me to remember the great value you see in me.

Teach me to take care of myself. Fill my spirit with your faithful love as I seek you first, each day. Help me to never harbor anger, discouragement, unforgiveness, or any other negative emotion, so my soul will be free. Teach me how to set boundaries of self-respect, not allowing others to cross lines they should not cross.

Thank you for loving me; I will do the same.

Expectancy

Praise forever Jehovah God, the God of Israel!
He is the one and only God of wonders,
surpassing every expectation.

Psalm 72:18

God, because of your love for me, I live in a continual state of expectancy. My aim is to be a glass-half-full type of person, always believing the best. You are with me and for me and have a good future planned for me.

I expect all of your promises to come to pass in my life, because you are faithful. Even when things are rough and I'm tempted to give up, hope is the fuel that ignites me and keeps me going. Instead of complaining, help me to find things to be joyful about. Help me to keep my mind set upon you. By your grace, I will win every battle.

I believe goodness and mercy follow me all the days of my life. Peace, health, provision, and blessings in abundance are drawn to me like a magnet. The relationships in my life become more and more enjoyable every day, because you bless them. Wisdom leads me, your presence protects me, and faith anchors me. I can't wait to see the great things you have in store for me today!

Strong in Battle

You've trained me with the weapons of warfare-worship;
now I'll descend down into battle with power
to chase and conquer my foes.

Psalm 18:34

Your Word has taught me well. Your love has emboldened me. In the middle of the fiercest battle, my arms are lifted high in praise. I know where my help comes from; it comes from you.

My eyes will remain fixed on you, even when the crashing waves threaten to tear apart the boat. You teach me the ways of rest, so I can sleep through the storm. Even when I cannot sense your presence, you are here with me. Your love steadies me. You strengthen me with joy that contradicts the chaos all around.

I believe in your love and trust in your goodness. The enemy doesn't stand a chance when I fight from my knees with a worshiping heart. My lips will declare your truth, wielding a blow that destroys every opposition. When I live for you, nothing is wasted. Even this trial will become the foundation for future victories. Through it, I get to know you like I never have. I discover your faithfulness in the midst of pain.

Flourish

Look how you've made all your lovers to flourish like palm trees,
each one growing in victory, standing with strength!
You've transplanted them into your heavenly courtyard
where they are thriving before you.

Psalm 92:12–13

Every day is filled with possibilities when I'm with you. You have filled me with your abundant life and caused me to flourish like a beautiful palm. I thrive in your presence, becoming all you've created me to be.

My life has become a flourishing garden. I am rooted and grounded in the soil of your love. Take me deeper. You have seated me beside you in heavenly places. Lift me higher. I want to know you more. I want to grow in grace.

You are my righteousness. As I live before you, I am transformed into your image. I don't even recognize myself as you take me from glory to glory. Your purifying work in my heart frees me to be all you've called me to be. You have become my victory!

Endless Possibilities

You satisfy my every desire with good things.
You've supercharged my life so that I soar again
like a flying eagle in the sky!

Psalm 103:5

Thank you for the way you bless me. You delight in surprising me with lovely things. You're the hope that fills me, even when things look bleak. When I focus on you, I'm filled with optimism—my glass isn't half full, it overflows!

The dreams inside of me come to life when I share them with you. You always encourage me and remind me everything is possible when it's done with you. I am confident that my future is brimming with promise. My life is in your hands. The possibilities are endless!

I set my mind on heavenly things and seek you first, knowing you will take care of the details. I will not be dismayed when stormy clouds come; instead, I will soar above them and see with the eyes of faith. You have touched me, strengthened me, and given me wisdom and energy to do all that is in my heart. You continually take me from glory to glory. The older I get, the better I feel!

Your Voice

Now I'll listen carefully for your voice
and wait to hear whatever you say.
Let me hear your promise of peace—
the message every one of your godly lovers longs to hear.
Just don't let us in our ignorance turn back from following you.

Psalm 85:8

When you speak to me, everything changes. My entire world becomes lighter—less precarious. Your voice releases peace, unlocking the chains of stress and illuminating the darkened corners of my life.

Help me to quiet my soul, so I can hear you more clearly. I yearn for the whispers that inflame my being, but I also long for thunderous roars of majesty. When you sing your songs of love over me, I sense it in every cell.

Counsel me with your perfect wisdom and infuse me with confidence as I follow your instructions. May I never follow the voice of a stranger. When you knock upon the door of my heart, may I answer immediately, never overthinking.

As I lay my head to rest at night, fill my dreams with divine conversations and glorious illustrations of your love. When the sunlight wakes the dawn, pierce my heart with your revelation. I'm listening, Lord. Speak to me.

Rays

Let the sunrise of your love end our dark night.
Break through our clouded dawn again!
Only you can satisfy our hearts,
filling us with songs of joy to the end of our days.
Psalm 90:14

Your love is like a ray of hope shining through the dark clouds. It warms my soul and brings me hope. Your face shines with glory into every situation. Just a glimpse of your smile sets my soul ablaze.

I want to experience you continually. Taste your profound love that is undeniably real. Your presence fulfills every longing of my soul. The riches of this world could never satisfy—you are the treasure I seek.

No matter what the day holds, I know you've got my back. You never leave me to fend for myself. Your wisdom is always available, if I only believe. You awaken my heart when it sleeps the sleep of despondency.

My soul is teaming with songs of love. Even in the midst of adversity, you bring melodies to life and remind me to sing. Worshiping you is one of my greatest pleasures. Joy bubbles within me, just by thinking about how much you love me!

Discover

When you sit enthroned under the shadow of Shaddai,
you are hidden in the strength of God Most High.

Psalm 91:1

I'm at my best when I'm walking with you. Facets of my character and gifts that have remained dormant come alive as you stir my soul. The glory of your presence builds my faith. I have absolute assurance that you are who you say you are.

As I allow myself to truly let go—spirit, soul, and body—all stress is replaced by your peace. I discover aspects of who you are within me when I hide myself in you. You become the strength within me and the joy that floods my being. I am the best version of me when I tuck myself away within the safety of your love and trust you unreservedly.

Give me glimpses into the vastness of who you are. I want to discover things about you that you've hidden up until now. I want to know you more than I know my closest friend. What a delight it is when you reveal your mysteries to me and show me how I fit into your great big plan. What an honor it is to be yours.

Open Arms

Lord, keep pouring out your unfailing love
on those who are near you.
Release more of your blessings
to those who are loyal to you.

Psalm 36:10

God, you fill me with wonder. You call my name and fill me with your grace. I'm overcome when I think of the many ways such a beautiful Savior reaches out to me. Your love is outrageous. It never stops and I've done nothing to earn it.

I love to feel your presence wooing me; drawing me near. I want nothing more than to run into your open arms. I can never get enough of your unfailing love. Show me your face. Open my eyes so I can see you more clearly. Open my ears and bless me with the sweetness of your voice. Breathe the breath of hope and blow away all shadow of doubt.

Your love flows like fragrant oil—it's the scent of love that flows from your very being. It floods my soul with the expectation of your glory. I am here, in your presence, and there is nothing in the world that can compare. My heart is soaring with thankfulness and joy.

Always Present

No matter where I am, even when I'm far from home,
I will cry out to you for a Father's help.
When I'm feeble and overwhelmed by life,
guide me into your glory where I am safe and sheltered.

Psalm 61:2

Lord, you constantly astound me. Your love is available and present in every situation I find myself in. From the most glorious times of worship, to the caves of darkest fears, you are with me.

I've known you in the joyful times and I've felt your presence when I'm bowed low with pain. You've taught me things during storms that I couldn't have learned any other way. I've learned how much you love me by the trials you've brought me through. The beauty of your faithfulness shines brightest in the gloomiest of valleys. You have always been there for me, even when you haven't said a word.

I choose to live each day in the shelter of your glory, which is always available. Your love empowers me to live in victory. No matter what I face, knowing how much you care for me gives me the courage to face another day.

Life Worth Imitating

I will follow [God's] commands and never stop.
I'll not sin by ceasing to follow him no matter what.
For I've kept my eyes focused on his righteous words
and I've obeyed everything that he's told me to do.

Psalm 18:21–22

I want to live a life worth imitating. A life of unquenchable devotion and obedience to your every word. I want love to be the driving force behind all I do and say.

May those who know me best witness my commitment to you, especially during the hardest times. Let them not just see my love for you, but feel how much I care about them. May they experience the tangible glory of your affection through me.

I don't want to live for myself, but to run with passion after you. I long to live in the absolute fullness of your resurrection power. You have called me to rise and shine and be a light to others. May I go forth with unselfish zeal and follow your example of doing all you saw the Father do. My life is not my own, for you have ignited my heart with passion to live for you.

Your Great Love

[God's people] forgot his great love,
how he took them by his hand
and with redemption's kiss
he delivered them from their enemies.

Psalm 78:42

Lord, help me to never forget how faithful you are. When I get sidetracked by worry and doubt, remind me of the many times you've come through for me. It's so easy to be distracted by trials when I turn my attention to the problem, instead of keeping my focus on you.

I relinquish the right to fear. The truth is, I can't do anything about many of the problems I face—only you can. All you ask is that I trust you and believe. You will come with redemption's kiss and deliver me, just as you have so many times before.

In the midst of the storm, I will declare your goodness and remember you're with me. Your Word will accomplish all you've sent it out to do. It will not return to you void. Every situation that was meant to harm me you will turn around for my good, simply because you love me. Believing in your great love for me is the key to unshakable faith.

No Holding Back

At the very moment I called out to you, you answered me!
You strengthened me deep within my soul
and breathed fresh courage into me.

Psalm 138:3

Nothing is too hard for you, God. And because you live inside of me, nothing is too hard for me either. When I'm faced with challenges, you strengthen me. You've given me everything I need to overcome.

I am courageous—bold as a lion. With you, I can face insecurities and fears and not let them stop me. Together we conquer every fear. You are with me everywhere I go. I won't live so safely that I never risk failure. I'm going to run after my dreams with you by my side.

Some of my goals may seem lofty and out of reach, but when I talk to you about them, you always encourage me to follow my heart. I'm not going to back down from things I've never done before. Even if I fail, I will not be defeated. I will try again and again until I succeed or you point me in a different direction. My victory will encourage others.

Life with you is often a wild ride—the adventures you've called me on are often far beyond my comfort zone. You aren't afraid of my mistakes and I won't be either. I won't let the fear of failure hold me back.

Believe

*Even when it seems I'm surrounded
by many liars and my own fears,
and though I'm hurting in my suffering and trauma,
I still stay faithful to God and I speak words of faith.*

Psalm 116:10–11

Lord, in the midst of turmoil and fear, give me unwavering faith. Demolish every fear with your powerful love. I let go of every thought that tries to make my problems look bigger than you. Nothing is too hard for you. Nothing.

I believe. In the areas where I struggle with unbelief, I ask for your mercy. I'll stand and declare your promises, letting them penetrate deep into my heart, so they become life within me. I remind myself of the many times you've come through for me before. You've never forgotten me, and even when it feels as if you have, I'll shake off the lie and lean into your love.

I release control and the need to understand. I seek you for wisdom and trust that if there's anything you want me to do besides believe, you'll show me. I refuse to worry. I was created to trust you and be at peace. Give me eyes to see this situation the way you do.

You'll get me through this. You love me. Faith gives me the victory.

Forever

May your tender love overwhelm me, O Lord,
for you are my Savior and you keep your promises.
Psalm 119:41

I come before you, laying every distraction at your feet. I love you. I need your presence more than anything else in this world. May my words of love move your heart. May my desire to walk the path of love bless you.

You draw me out of religion's box and into your chambers. Your love is all the motivation I need to live a life of purity and holiness. I run with arms wide open into the house I now call home. Your presence is my safe haven; the one place I can be myself. I'm honored you've brought me near.

I want to eat and drink of you and become all you've created me to be. I want to stay here, in the reality of your glory, always. I am lovesick, ruined for the lesser things of earthly life. Let me live in the awareness of your overwhelming love forever.

The Outpouring of Revelation

The Lord is my Revelation Light to guide me along the way;
he's the Source of my salvation to defend me every day.
I fear no one!
I'll never turn back and run from you, Lord,
surround and protect me.

Psalm 27:1

Your revelations illuminate the very core of my being. They strengthen me with hope and guide my steps. They're the source of my salvation, which led me to you. By them, I discover the promises for a prosperous life and the path to happiness.

God, you're always there for me. Your words still the tremors of fear when the enemy attacks. Even if an entire army comes against me, you offer me peace in place of terror. All I have to do is choose to trust you.

I want to live my life close to you—tucked within the very secrets of your heart. Discovering the endless brilliance of your glorious truths. Hide me away here—in the center of your holiness. Fill me with awe as I gaze upon the sweetness of your face.

Yes, all of your revelations lead me to you.

The Joy of Discovery

*Lord, direct me throughout my journey
so I can experience your plans for my life.
Reveal the life-paths that are pleasing to you.*

Psalm 25:4

What an honor it is to walk with you through life. How kind and generous you are—the very essence of agape love. You are always here, always willing to listen, and ever true. As you whisper your secrets to me, I discover you, not only as Lord and King, but Friend.

Together we run through the field of my dreams and you lift me up and twirl me around, filling my ears with laughter. This beautiful place was created for my pleasure and I never have to fear that I'm dreaming too big. With you, the joy of my heart is unleashed and I'm free to discover with you.

The journey of life takes me through many winding roads, but as long as I follow you, I will never veer from the path that pleases you. I want to experience your plans for my life and to discover my true purpose. All my days, I will sing of your goodness. You are the way.

King of My Heart

Wake up, you living gateways!
Lift up your heads, you ageless doors of destiny!
Welcome the King of Glory,
for he is about to come through you.

Psalm 24:7

King of Glory, you are welcome in my life. I awaken to your knock upon my heart and I reply with full abandon. Come! I open the gates of my soul to your holy presence. Dwell within me and never leave.

Mighty God, invincible in every way, you have conquered my heart. Your resurrection power fills me, so that I can stand my ground even in the thick of battle. You have given me everything I need to defeat the forces that oppose me. The enemy flees when he sees me coming. I can't help but laugh because I'm wearing your armor—I look a lot like you!

You are the King of my heart, whose every word nourishes my entire being. Holy One, I bow before your majesty, rejoicing in your eternal victory. Unfold the triumph of your glory in my life.

The Beauty of the Cross

I'm surrounded by many violent foes. ...
They have pierced my hands and my feet.
Like a pack of wild dogs they tear at me,
swirling around me with their hatred.
They gather around me like lions to pin my hands and feet.
Psalm 22:12, 16

Thank you for the cross. For the love that held you there, so that I could be free. As I kneel before your holy presence, I'm reminded of the suffering you endured all because you love me.

The beauty of the cross has awakened me to life. You've torn down the walls of separation and restored love's connection. You've brought me near. Love flowed freely that day, so many years ago on Calvary. The sacrifice of love became eternity's most powerful victory.

Beautiful King, words fail me, as I imagine the torture you endured. The precious blood that spilled upon the shackles of the soon-to-be-redeemed became Yahweh's most precious gift. Though the cross held one Man—heaven and earth's Sovereign King—there was room enough for all humankind. A most horrid scene became the beauty of the ages.

Help me to never forget the unfathomable price of love. I am the joy that was set before you. You did it for me. Thank you.

Abundant Love

Lord, ... the comfort of your love takes away my fear.
I'll never be lonely, for you are near.
You become my delicious feast
even when my enemies dare to fight.

Psalm 23:4–5

My heart overflows in the presence of your love. Even in the midst of my enemies, you revive me with the fragrance of your Holy Spirit and teach me to trust. As I rest in your strong arms, you restore my soul.

Your love is extravagant. It crashes upon me in torrents of never-ending bliss, until my every breath responds. I want to discover the vast expanse of this love—to swim its depths and soar its heights. Fall fresh upon me each day and give me all I can drink of your presence, until I am left wanting nothing else. Come, sweep me off my feet anytime you want!

Teach me to remain aware of you at all times. Tutor me in the ways of this selfless love. As I journey through life, guide me with your eye, so I will never stray. You're the culmination of all my hopes and dreams. Lord, you're my greatest reality.

Because of You

Lord, because of your strength the king is strong.
Look how he rejoices in you!
He bursts out with a joyful song because of your victory!

Psalm 21:1

What joy I have found in this life of faith! What victory I partake of, because of you! Blessing after blessing chases me down as I yield to your holy ways. You are the God of glory and honor, the Lord of abounding mercy and endless truth. You clothe me in splendor and anoint me with endless grace.

Because of you, I can soar above the clouds of discouragement, dive into the oceans of joy, or simply stand my ground. You are the courage that fills me as I roar with holy boldness. Because of you, fear has faced its final hour. I'm no longer its prisoner.

You are the strength to believe when doubt is screaming in my face. You're my source of peace and my reason to worship. Because of you, I'm beautiful. You call me your own and have made me worthy. Because of you, life is an adventure. Because of you, I'm free!

I Choose

Some find their strength in their weapons and wisdom,
but my miracle deliverance can never be won by men.
Our boast is in the Lord our God who
makes us strong and gives us victory!

Psalm 20:7

I choose to believe! Lord, fill me with your perfect love that drives away all fear. Remind me of your faithfulness in times past and the glorious future yet to come. Teach me to frame my world with your unwavering promises and bring every thought captive to your truth. Nothing can overwhelm me when I listen to you.

I choose faith and deny fear a place in my heart. I choose to seek you before anything else and to keep you as the center of my focus. You are good. You are faithful; never failing. You're all I ever need—the answer to every question and every trial. God of more than enough, you delight in sharing the abundance of your house with me.

When I go through the fire, you teach me to dance in the flames. You teach me the sounds of joy by laughing at my enemies. Even in the midst of my adversaries, my cup overflows. With lifted hands and joyful heart, I choose you and you're more than enough. You are the God of miracles who promises me victory!

Holy Vessels

They are passionate and wholehearted,
always sincere and always speaking the truth—
for their hearts are trustworthy.

Psalm 15:2

God, I want to live in the place where your glory abides. Fill me with your Spirit. You in me and I in you. This is the place of perfection, where spirit and soul collide in the never-ending expanse of love.

Saturate every dark crevice of my soul with the light of your glory. Strip me of everything that doesn't look like you; beautify me with your presence. May my thoughts flow in unity with yours—teaming with faith and free from fear. Refine me with your holy fire, so that all that is within me echoes your holiness.

You're my passionate pursuit, my treasure, and my delight. I follow after you with wholehearted desire, no longer living for myself. Let your favor rest upon me, so that it's seen everywhere I go. Set me apart as your holy vessel and let the overflow of your Spirit empower those around me.

May my words reflect your heart and carry your nature. When people look at me, let them see you instead.

November

Promises Delayed

I'm hurting, Lord—will you forget me forever?
How much longer, Lord?
Psalm 13:1

Breathe your life into my dreams. It seems they have vanished like a passing vapor. I held them once, in my hands, but fear stole them away. Instead, I should have enclosed them in my heart, anchored within your presence.

Lord, please don't make me wait much longer. Make a way, because there seems to be no way. Let me see the paths you once showed me. Encourage me, so that faith will rise again. You are the Holy One—not a man who can lie. What you have promised, you will bring to pass.

I love you enough to accept the apparent contradiction that this season brings. Though the road to seeing your promises come to pass seems obscure, you will illuminate it with your glory and wisdom. Kneeling before you now, I declare, "Not my will, but yours be done." I choose to trust in your perfect timing and rest in your faithfulness. Hope comes alive when I hide myself in you.

The Righteous Ones

Help, Lord! Save us! For godly ones are swiftly disappearing.
Where are the dependable, principled ones?
They're a vanishing breed!
Psalm 12:1

The world looks different through your eyes, Lord. Though darkness seems to have infiltrated so many aspects of society, I see the light that shines in its midst. You remain, glistening through your chosen vessels, as we learn to walk in righteousness. We're the shining ones, whose words are true and whose prayers are answered.

Lord, I dedicate myself to you—every part. My heart is committed to be one of these righteous ones. Purify my thoughts as I bring each one to you. Let every action be fueled with passion for holiness. May every part of me flow in unison with your Holy Spirit, as together we run to fulfill your words upon the earth.

I stand before you, righteous. Not because of anything I have done or could ever do, but because of what you've already done. You're my true example of compassion and selflessness. I devote myself to follow the paths that lead to godliness and virtue, bringing honor to your name.

In Times of Criticism

The Eternal One is never shaken—
he is still found in his temple of holiness
reigning as Lord and King over all.
He is closely watching everything that happens.
And with a glance, his eyes examine every heart.
For his heavenly rule will prevail over all.

Psalm 11:4

Lord, you see everything that happens. You're aware of those who gossip and slander my name. The surging waters of criticism are trying to drown me, but you've asked me not to resist, but to learn to float. Knowing your arms of protection will hold me, I can rest.

Eternal One, you are never shaken by wickedness. You love what is right and just. You detest evil and won't allow it to destroy me. Swallow these lies with the light of your love. Restore me. I am fully dependent upon you.

Every heart is exposed to your searching gaze. The righteous and the wicked will both answer to you. Though I want to defend myself, I choose to have faith in your deliverance. I give up my right to argue and my desire to make people believe the truth about me. You know me and that is enough. Your righteousness will prevail.

The Children

Lord, your name is so great and powerful! ...
You have built a stronghold by the songs of babies.
Strength rises up with the chorus of singing children.
This kind of praise has the power to shut Satan's mouth.
Childlike worship will silence
the madness of those who oppose you.

Psalm 8:1–2

Not through the seraphim or cherubim, but from babies and children, have you perfected praise. Father, thank you for these little ones—these examples of abandoned love and zealous devotion. Faithfully, you remind us what it's like to be free from anxiety and cares, to trust you wholeheartedly. Their joyful praise silences the mouth of the enemy.

Bless the children with divine protection. Guard them—spirit, soul, and body. Draw them ever closer to you, so they'll never stray. Let hope and faith be their close friends. May they never get stuck in laws of religion, but remain free to experience the awe of encountering you. Fill them with wisdom and grace. May fearlessness, compassion, and wisdom equip them to transform the world.

Fill your children of every age with childlike faith and joyful anticipation. Thank you for reminding us what it's like to be your child. May we never lose the fascination of life with you.

Touch

I'm so exhausted and worn-out with my weeping.
I endure weary, sleepless nights filled with moaning,
soaking my pillow with my tears.

Psalm 6:6

Extend your hand to me, Lord. I need your merciful touch. Weariness has gripped me and won't let go. I'm exhausted— my nights are filled with weeping. I don't know where you've gone or when you will return. But I know you love me. Please don't make me wait much longer.

My eyes of faith won't focus anymore. Turn to me and hear my thunderous cry. Speak a word and heal my wounded soul. My speech cannot convey what burns within my heart, so I'll sit in silence and wait.

You love me. You will come.

The rhythm of my breath begins to flow with the cadence of peace I once knew. Melodies of hope rise within, swallowing the doubt that was eating me away. I lean into the faint brush of your nearness. At last, you have come. Now all things will be made right again.

I Know the Way

I know the way back home,
and I know that you will welcome me into your house,
for I am covered by your covenant of mercy and love.
So I come to your sanctuary with deepest awe
to bow in worship and adore you.

Psalm 5:7

Lord, why are you silent? Though I can feel you here, my heart yearns to hear your voice. These incessant thoughts drown you out; the busyness of life fights for my attention. I need your grace, so I can slow down, still my mind, and focus on you. At times it seems a losing battle, but I know you won't relent in drawing me.

My spirit groans for the love I once knew. I haven't lost my way, but I feel dry. Quick run-ins with your presence aren't enough. I need encounters with your love—constantly. Visit me with words that flow from your heart, so my soul awakens. Take me over completely.

By faith I come. I know the way to your home—I've frequented the path. Your covenant of mercy and love have paved the way, and I run with abandon back into your arms. Now nothing else matters than to be with you. Sometimes your touch is louder than words.

Empowered by Love

You empower me for victory with
your wrap-around presence.
Your power within makes me strong to subdue,
and by stooping down in gentleness
you strengthened me and made me great!

Psalm 18:35

Empower me with your magnificent strength. Together we will leap over walls and scale the highest mountains. No longer will I identify with the stronghold of fear. Instead, courage will define me. In you, I am bolder than a lion.

I have witnessed your power when you rescued me from the midst of the enemy's camp. Now I know that nothing could ever stop your love. It is a mighty force; a storm of burning coals. Many waters could never quench it.

Life with you is exhilarating! Your presence makes me great. It's the victory that overcomes every sin and the strength of joy within me. Together we laugh in the face of our enemies. I will trust in you forever and shout praises for all you've done and are yet to do. Your love is my victory!

The Treasure of Your Love

I've kept my integrity by surrendering to him.
And so the Lord has rewarded me with his blessing.
This is the treasure I discovered
when I kept my heart clean before his eyes.

Psalm 18:24

Your love is a treasure chest filled with blessing. I dive into its bounty and rise with hands and heart overflowing with riches. Nothing satisfies like the abundance of your love. No one fills me with hope the way that you do.

You're everything to me—life's greatest joy. I'm the wealthiest person alive, because I live within your glory. You bring salvation, health, provision, and peace. You're the answer to every prayer I've ever prayed. You fill me with wisdom and strength, shining the spotlight on fear, so it cannot hide.

Your enduring love lasts forever. It is more valuable than the rarest of jewels. It beautifies me and makes me whole. Worthy Lord, I want to know the height and depth of its extent and swim in the midst of its waters.

Purify Me

I've done my best to be blameless
and to follow all his ways,
keeping my heart pure.

Psalm 18:23

God, I consecrate myself to you. I'm open to your searching gaze. Purify me, so I'll look and act like you. Keep my heart from doing wrong. Let integrity keep me and holiness define me.

In humility I come before you to declare your perfecting power. You breathe upon my soul and decorate it with ornaments of grace. Your mercy always leads me to truth. You're my delight and the code I willingly embrace.

I live for you. I acknowledge your lordship in my life. Let the meditations of my heart echo the excellence that abides within. For you know my thoughts, even those I try to hide. Illuminate my soul and let there be light in every word I speak. Fill me with your glory and burn away anything that still looks like me. Ignite the fires of your love ... everywhere I go.

Experiencing His Word

God's Word is perfect in every way;
how it revives our souls!
His laws lead us to truth,
and his ways change the simple into wise.

Psalm 19:7

God, I love your Word. It revives my soul and makes my spirit shine. Its revelation brings the path of life into view, guiding my steps with perfect vision. Your Word is alive, filling me with hope for each new day.

I am fed by its wisdom—the very wisdom that's been with you since the beginning of time. It sustains me more than my daily bread. Your Word teaches me how to pray, what to believe, and how to speak. It's my constant encouragement. This Word is a sword, cutting away what's not of you; dividing between darkness and light.

Intertwine your Word into every thought, every pattern of belief. I don't just want to *know* it's true, I want to *experience* its faithfulness until it becomes a river flowing within me. Establish me now, in your truth, as I hide your promises in my heart.

The Beautiful God of Grace

In your day of danger may the Lord answer and deliver you!
May the name of the God of Grace
set you safely on high!

Psalm 20:1

You are the God of grace. You empower me for a life of victory, strengthening me for whatever lies ahead. Thank you for the beautiful gift of grace in my life. It is the expression of joy and the enablement for every good work. As I follow the pathways of grace and obey your Word, you unlock the blessings of heaven and lavish them upon me.

I can do all things when I walk with you. In the midst of difficulties, your grace abounds. Though I'm struck down, I will not give up! Instead, I will press into your presence and embrace your grace. It's the treasure of endurance within me and the power to overcome.

Your grace enables me to become all you've created me to be—to live a life of glorious success and patient perseverance. Wrap me in a cocoon of unending strength and favor, so that everywhere I go, others will see your goodness and be drawn to your love. Nothing compares to this undeserved gift!

The Bliss of His Presence

Lord, because of your strength the king is strong. ...
Your victory heaps blessing after blessing upon him.
What joy and bliss he tastes, rejoicing before your face!

Psalm 21:1, 6

Your victory has brought me near. The sting of death has been swallowed by the joy of life in you. Faithful God, none can compare to you! Your almighty arms scoop me up and hold me tight. I will not resist this holy embrace.

With unveiled face I behold your glory. Rivers of living water flow from your throne and rainbows of color stream from your heart. Oh the blissfulness of your presence! I long for words to articulate your beauty. Your eyes blaze with passion I've never known. Your holiness is so pure, I can barely stand.

You call me closer, but at times your touch is more than I can handle. Anoint me with strength, so I'll not perish before your divine presence. I'm overwhelmed by this blessing of divine love.

The Beauty of Silence

Each day gushes out its message to the next,
night with night whispering its knowledge to all.
Without a sound, without a word,
without a voice being heard.

Psalm 19:2–3

In the stillness, you are here. You don't speak a word, yet the reality of your love is louder than a million voices. My thoughts are quiet; I feel you—breathing life into the depths of my spirit.

Your glory shines through the darkness that surrounds me, rising on the horizon of my heart. You touch me with the vibrancy of a brilliant sunrise. Come closer. Share your secrets with me. Teach me to soar above the clouds, where all I can hear is the sweetness of your love.

You're as radiant as a bridegroom on his wedding day. You don't need to say a word, for when you look at me with those eyes of zealous love, I'm overcome. This feels like a dream. The King of the universe has chosen me!

I surrender in holy worship, leaning into your embrace. Now, the only sound I hear is the beating of a lovesick heart— yours and mine. Tangled knots of tangible affection. You're the beauty of silence.

Peace

Now I'll lie down and go to sleep—
and I'll awake in safety for you surround me with your glory.
Even though dark powers prowl around me,
with their words like sharp arrows, I won't be afraid.

Psalm 3:5–6

Lord, bring me into your loving embrace and leave me there. Still the thoughts churning through my troubled mind. Where questions loom, diffuse the fragrance of your peace. Restore my courage as I learn to trust in you completely. I relinquish the right to understand.

Surround me with yourself, so I cannot feel the rush of violent winds blowing from the enemy's camp. In the darkest of valleys, you remain with me. Though hidden in obscurity, the radiance of your face reveals heaven's path. You always make a way.

You're the invisible God, yet I see you clearly as you live inside my heart. Move me with the breath of your Spirit, lest I heed the foolishness of my limited understanding.

With all of my worries and anxieties surrendered into your care, I rest in your arms. Cover me with a blanket of peace and I will lie down and sleep, unafraid of what tomorrow holds.

My Messiah

"I will reveal the eternal purpose of God.
For he has decreed over me, 'You are my favored Son.
And as your Father I have crowned you as my King Eternal.
Today I became your Father.'"

Psalm 2:7

Jesus, you reveal God's eternal purpose. You're the Messiah; God's eternal King. I honor the beauty of your holy name. You're my magnificent salvation; the One who took away my curse. My greatest desire is to know you more.

Fear was conquered when you filled me with your love. Gently you held the torn pages of my life and sewed them back together with threads of blood-bought glory. The power of your resurrection surges through me—spirit, soul, and body. I am but a shadow of who I used to be, now that I've come alive in you.

The very substance of your love triumphed over death. Now I live face-to-face with the One my heart loves. You've uncaged the joy that was once held prisoner within me. Miracles still flow from your nail-scarred hands. I should know—I am one of those miracles.

It is finished and you did it for me, your bride. This is love. This is our story.

Love's Revelation

What delight comes to those who follow God's ways! ...
Their pleasure and passion is remaining true
to the Word of "I Am," meditating day
and night in his true revelation of light.

Psalm 1:1–2

Lord, wholeheartedly and without reservation, I am yours. I bow before you now and invite you to be the King of my heart. Revive me with your holy kisses. Sustain me with your love, for one moment without you is far too long.

When I thought it wasn't possible, you blazed your way through the walls I had built, and conquered my heart with your love. Now I stand firm in the light of this revelation: You love me and will never leave me. You are faithful, even when I am not.

I see you now—face-to-face with the One my heart loves. Oh, how I love your face! Tend to the garden of my heart; awaken it day by day with your tender whispers that ignite my soul. My passion is to remain true to the great, "I Am."

Living with you is indescribable joy; the fulfillment of every dream. You've captured me with your love and I will never let you go! This is the revelation of love.

I Need You

As I thought of you I just moaned: "God, where are you?"
I'm overwhelmed with despair as I wait for your help to arrive.
I can't get a wink of sleep until you come and comfort me.
Now I'm too burdened to even pray!

Psalm 77:3–4

All I can do is sit in your presence. My heart is broken. I've never felt pain so deeply before. One of the worst things imaginable has happened, and I don't even know how to pray. I need you. My mind is swirling with more thoughts than I can keep up with.

Come and be with me. Hold me. Strengthen me. Comfort me. I'm falling apart. I'm empty. In the midst of this destruction all I can do is choose to believe.

I see you now, dressing in battle array. You are my Champion—you'll fight for me, but you're calling me to find courage and fight with you. I offer you my worship and my trust, even in the midst of the fear that tries to kill me.

I speak light into the darkness. I pull on your promises, God. You are faithful. All I can do is lift my hands and offer you the sacrifice of praise. You're the way, the truth, and the life. In you, I'm more than a conqueror. I will not be defeated!

I Trust You

Every one of your godly lovers receives
even more than what they ask for.
For you hear what their hearts really long for
and you bring them your saving strength!

Psalm 145:19

Your promises anchor my soul. I believe in you. I trust you. Though storms rage and the enemy hisses in my ear, I remain tethered to your heart. Counsel me with your love and I'll never fear.

Rising within me is the truth of your word. I am royalty. I won't forget who I am and to whom I belong. I am yours and you are mine. You will never forsake me. Your very nature is revealed in the way you care for me. You are tender, kind, and all-powerful.

I see you peering through the lattice; your gaze rests upon my heart. Come closer. Fight for me. Make a way. Weave yourself into the dark webs of doubt and unbelief, so nothing remains but the light of hope. Though I cry out for one thing, give me what I truly need. I lift my prayer to you and leave it in your hands.

Bubbling Over

Our hearts bubble over as we celebrate the fame
of your marvelous beauty, bringing bliss to our hearts.
We shout with ecstatic joy over your breakthrough for us.

Psalm 145:7

Lord, you are beautiful! My heart explodes with gratitude, for your tender love is seen in everything you do. From now throughout eternity, your praise will flow effortlessly from my lips. You're everything to me.

Your open hands are filled with blessings, which you lavish upon me. I don't deserve your kindness, yet you paint my world with grace. How beautifully patient you are—never disqualifying me because of my weaknesses. I shout with joy over your faithfulness toward me.

Nothing can steal this joy. No one can take this peace from me, for you have given it as a gift. With eyes and heart fixed upon you, I discover your kingdom reigning within my heart and I bubble over with excitement! I can't keep it to myself. I know what I must do! I will tell the world of the wonders of your love and limitless power. You fill my world with bliss.

You Know Me

I thank you, God, for making me so mysteriously complex!
Everything you do is marvelously breathtaking.
It simply amazes me to think about it!
How thoroughly you know me, Lord!

Psalm 139:14

I am here, Lord, before your presence with nothing to hide. I submit myself to you fully. You are more intimately acquainted with me than anyone I know. You read my heart like an open book and handle it with the utmost care. I want you, with no space between us. I want to see the beauty of your face and smell the fragrance of your presence.

You've loved me before I ever saw the light of day. When you created me in the secret place and formed me out of the substance of love, you took delight in me. You saw who I was destined to be, before I was born. There is nothing hidden from the One who shaped my delicate inside and my intricate outside. How simply amazing that is! It is precious and wonderful to consider.

Even now you are with me. I feel your gaze upon my heart. May every word, every thought, and every act be pleasing to you—filled with the very essence of Christ. Thank you for loving me so well. I am yours—completely.

Your Love

Wherever I go, your hand will guide me;
your strength will empower me.

Psalm 139:10

I feel your hand of love upon my life—guiding me, protecting me, loving me. In every season you're with me, as my Friend, my Lord, my Healer. When I'm weak, you strengthen me. When I'm happy, you're the reason I sing.

Your love surrounds me—never leaves me. There is nowhere I could flee from your Spirit, nor is there any place I could hide from your face. You are everywhere. In the center of the blazing sun or in the realm of the dead—you are there waiting. You will find me and bring me back to you.

Thank you for the way you cherish me. I am more confident in your love for me than anything else in this world. You see past my words and into the very movement of my heart and soul. You understand my every thought before I think it. When I'm with you, everything is clear. Your love is heaven on earth.

I Will Fly

How could we sing the song of the Lord
in this foreign wilderness?

Psalm 137:4

Lord, teach me to be free—to soar higher than my circumstances. Only you can release me from these doubts and fears that hold me captive. I have nothing to offer you besides my love and devotion. Nothing left to wrap my hands around other than you.

Blow your awakening breath of change. Lift me higher above this desert land and teach me to fly. I will lift my hands and sing my songs of thankfulness. You're all I have. And in truth, you're all I need. I will choose to smile and lay my questions at your feet. You are my hope. You are faithful. You dance with me in the midst of the fire. You love me.

Every day I will choose you. This is what will define me. This is the legacy I will leave—a heart of undivided devotion regardless of temporary struggles. You are close to the brokenhearted. Nothing can separate me from your love.

Speechless

Give thanks to the great God of the heavens!
His tender love for us continues on forever!

Psalm 136:26

God, you are good! I stand in awe of your great wisdom that fills the heavens. You light the skies with reflections of your glory—the sun to brighten the day, the moon and stars to guard the night. How glorious you are! It stirs me to praise!

As I walk along the water's edge and gaze into the horizon, I'm reminded of your powerful words that separated the land and sea and obey you still. Birds of the air and fish in the water's depths follow your voice and are sustained. How mighty you are!

Yet, despite the many beautiful things you made, I am your greatest treasure. You chose me as your very own—to be the temple of your holy presence. The great God of the heavens desires to be one with me. My heart is overcome. How unfathomable are your power, love, and tenderness! You have rendered me speechless.

Atoning Love

Your forgiving love is what makes you so wonderful.
No wonder you are loved and worshiped!
This is why I wait upon you, expecting your breakthrough,
for your word brings me hope.

Psalm 130:4–5

You're my new beginning. You ransomed me from the slavery of sin and washed me in your atoning love. Every part of me is open to you. There's nothing left to hide—you see it all. You know me. You love me.

I don't deserve your love. Even the smallest sin should separate me from you. Yet you call me worthy enough to die for and made provision for me to live before your throne forever. Close to you—experiencing the nearness of heaven on earth, even now. How tenderhearted you are. How merciful and kind. My Magnificent Redeemer—so forgiving.

Through the night, I wait upon you—yearning for one more encounter with your holy presence. I've never known love like this. It fills me with hope and overcomes the plague of doubt. You're everything I need—the foundation I build my life upon.

Content

I am humbled and quieted in your presence.
Like a contented child that rests on its mother's lap,
I'm your resting child and my soul is content in you.

Psalm 131:2

You wait for me in the stillness. I feel you tugging on my heart, and I respond with full surrender. I quiet my clamoring thoughts and turn all my attention to you. Touch my eyes that I may see you. Whisper the mysteries of your love that inflame my heart with longing.

If only I could grasp this passion that stirs within me and hold it in my hand. But no—love cannot be understood with the mind. It can only be enjoyed by the heart. It's your greatest gift—your very identity.

Here in your embrace, I'm completely fulfilled—like a baby resting in its mother's arms. I will emerge with answers to prayers that once consumed my soul, yet for now, nothing else seems to matter. This is the place where my greatest destiny is realized—to be with you.

Words cannot convey what burns within my heart, so I will sit in silence. Content in the wonder.

The Joy of Worship

How joyous are those who love the Lord
and bow low before God,
Ready to obey him!

Psalm 128:1

With joy-filled heart, I bow before you. You're my song, my dance—the celebration of my soul. You're the momentum that drives me forward with courageous faith. I'm overcome with gratefulness because of your constant gifts of tender devotion.

You lavish me with love that arrests my heart. I am ruined for anything else. You open my eyes and suddenly I view the world through different lenses. I see you in every sunrise and hear you in the wind. I see you in the eyes of the poor and in the touch of an orphan's hand. You're all around me.

I hear you beckoning me to come closer, eager to unfold the generosity of your reward to this lovesick bride. You set me free to worship you without restraint. I delight myself in you, for you fill me with happiness unlike anything I've ever known. Your love is so real. I am yours forever.

Sustained by Your Love

Let all Israel admit it.
From our very beginning we have been
persecuted by the nations.
And from our very beginning,
we have faced never-ending discrimination.
Nevertheless, our enemies have not defeated us.
We're still here!

Psalm 129:1–2

I'm still here. Darkness will not overtake me, because you are good! Your love sustains me through every trial. Your blessing has broken every chain. You are with me and I will forever be connected to your heart.

The scars of cutting words have turned to golden glory—each one healed by your kiss. Though persecution arises, you always stand by my side and defend me. When I'm broken and undone, you breathe life back into my soul. You will never let me down.

The world is filled with abstract commotion that seeks to distract me and arrest my thoughts. Instead, I will put the demands of my day on hold just to be with you. I will focus upon your empowering love. You're all I need. I'm sustained by your love.

Never Alone

It was like a dream come true
when you freed us from our bondage
and brought us back to Zion!
Psalm 126:1

Though I wander in the shadows, I'm not alone. You lead me with your quiet voice; all I have to do is lean in and listen. You are here. You restore me.

At times faith is my only friend—but what a beautiful friend she is. She holds my hand and reminds me of your redeeming love. You've rescued me and turned things around, more times than I can count. I've tasted of your faithfulness. I've known what it's like to experience breakthrough. You'll do it again.

Your love and light shine brighter than the darkness of this season. I can see it now—it pierces through the cracks and illuminates my soul. Though my heart is dry, I cling to you. Seeds of tears once scattered along the ground have become majestic trees where you refresh me with your tender care.

Suddenly, the path is clear. The way to freedom so evident—it's like a dream come true. My heart swells as I run with joyous laughter toward the answers you've always held.

Thank you.

Futility

It really is senseless to work so hard
from early morning till late at night,
toiling to make a living for fear of not having enough.
God can provide for his lovers, even while they sleep!

Psalm 127:2

God, I need your grace. I can't do this without you. I know—I've tried. I've done everything I can to make things go the way I want them to. Striving, toiling, doing everything I know to do, yet it amounts to nothing. It's all in vain and I repent.

You are my source of provision. There is nothing I need that you won't provide. You love me. My heart was torn because I wasn't trusting you. I was blinded by worry and anxiety, but then you came. You stripped the veils from my eyes and showed me the futility of fear and the power of love.

The fragrance of grace is released upon the winds. I can smell it. I can feel it blowing from heaven—cool and refreshing. You visit me with words that release my heart into freedom. Your love melts away my fear. I will rest in you. I trust you. I love you.

The Record
of Your Love

We can praise God over and over that he never left us!
God wouldn't allow the terror of our enemies to defeat us.

Psalm 124:6

Lord, I invite you into my past. Rewrite my history, so I find you in every story. Within each fleck of disappointment, uncover your greater purpose. For you have been my victory—my Shelter in every storm.

In the darkest of valleys, I beheld the power of your faithful love. When I discovered the shadows that hindered my faith, you were the One shining the light of truth. You smiled and held me close, knowing the strongholds of deception were being dismantled.

Walk with me in the garden; breathe life into the images that now bloom in my remembrance. Every season contains a record of your love with lessons to be learned. Each tear has become a fragrant flower—the scent of unyielding devotion. You are the author of my life—the glory of my past, the peace in the present, and the wisdom for the future. Your love is eternal.

December

I Love You

I long to drink of you, O God,
drinking deeply from the streams of pleasure
flowing from your presence.
My longings overwhelm me for more of you!

Psalm 42:1

My heart is streaming with this one theme—I love you.

You are holy, beautiful, the gift of unceasing mercy and grace. You're the joy that surprises me on dark paths and the praise that fills the spaces void of hope. You're the reason I wake and the blessing of peace while I sleep. You are the love that lives inside of me.

This is what I was made for—to delight in you. To drink of your intoxicating love, until I am completely overwhelmed and longing for more. I am addicted to the nearness of your presence. Permeate every cell of my being with your glory and never stop. Set me free from lesser loves.

Let my entire life be a gift of unending devotion—a pleasing offering poured out over and over again. I love you.

The Hope
of the Humble

*Lord, you know and understand all the hopes
of the humble and will hear their cries
and comfort their hearts, helping them all.*

Psalm 10:17

There is evil all around me. Darkness, which tries to intimidate and oppress. Yet in the midst of it, I endeavor to be like you—unshaken by those who spew forth lies and threats; undaunted by their boasts of calamity and destruction. Wickedness believes it's veiled beneath a cloud of obscurity, free to prey on the weak. But we know the truth—you see it all.

These calamities drive us to our knees and remind us of our great need for you. Lord, you're our Hiding Place—the hope of the humble. You hear the cry of the afflicted and comfort weary hearts, never fearing that your enemies will prevail. In you we trust, knowing you rule in righteousness from your holy temple. Bring the wicked to justice so your children will no longer be terrified or overwhelmed.

Let my life resemble yours, echoing your heart of compassion toward those who are broken and traumatized. May I defend the helpless, comfort the weary, and bring deliverance to the oppressed, radiating your love into every situation.

Wholly Yours

In a visitation of the night
you inspected my heart and refined my soul in fire
until nothing vile was found in me.
I've wanted my words and my ways to always agree.

Psalm 17:3

Lord, no one knows me the way you do. Though you see every motive and intent of my heart, I will stand before you and look you in the eye, embracing your holy fire as you refine my soul. You're my treasure, my delight, my mighty Savior.

Only by following your words have I been able to walk before you, innocent. The wonder of your mercy has molded me and I want nothing more than to honor you all the days of my life. Let my words and actions please you at all times. May no vile thing ever be found in me.

You are wonderful, attentive to my prayer. You give me freedom to run alongside of you, yet you always keep an eye on me like a loving parent. When evil rears its ugly head, I turn to hide myself in you. Pull me in and wrap your wings tightly around me, so those who desire to destroy me cannot find me.

You're my vindicator and I submit myself wholly to you.

Redeemer

Give victory to our king, O God!
The day we call on you, give us your answer!
Psalm 20:9

You are the King whose hands flow with mighty miracles. No one—whether by weapon, wisdom, or strength—can bring victorious redemption quite like you do. You're the God of grace who hears us when we pray and sends help from Zion.

Father, those who are weary and facing impossible situations need your strong hand to rescue them. Let their cries for deliverance be heard throughout heaven. Remember every sacrifice of love, every shout of praise, each gift they've lavished upon you, and in your great mercy grant the desires of their hearts.

We remain steadfast, knowing you are faithful to answer. Impart courage and strength to your beloved as we rise in celebration to bless your name. Our boast is in you and you alone.

Lord, unfold our triumph as a banner of victory. You make our dreams come true.

You Bore My Shame

*How could anyone be disgraced
when they've entwined their hearts with you?*

Psalm 25:3

There is no joy greater than the joy I find in you. Rich in mercy, you invite me to draw close, even though the sins of my immaturity should disqualify me. You're the God of my salvation and my heart is entwined with yours. To forever live before you in holy reverence is an honor I don't deserve.

When the humble turn to you, you joyfully welcome them and cast none away. You see everyone through the eyes of love and grace. May your mercy always steer me in the right direction, your truth guide me, and your love eternally surround me.

The path you've paved for me has been laid with love and faithfulness, and leads to favor and blessing. My burdens are lifted when I walk in the light of your truth. You have borne my shame. Take me by the hand and escort me on this beautiful journey of life.

My Greatest Joy

Lord, when you said to me, "Seek my face,"
my inner being responded:
I'm seeking your face with all my heart.

Psalm 27:8

Lord, I want to live from a posture of awe and wonder—so close to you that each of my prayers bring you delight. Abiding with you every moment of every day is one of the most remarkable privileges anyone could hope for, but that's my heartfelt desire—more than anything else in the whole world. May the deepest depths of my union with you be reflected in everything I say and do.

Thank you for hiding me in the shelter of your holiness. It's amazing how courageous I am with you protecting me. I'm afraid of nothing! No matter how close the enemy comes, when I'm with you in the secret place of your glory, he can't touch me.

You told me to seek your face, and with longing unlike I've ever known, I've been seeking you ever since. You brought me into your family when others abandoned me and you've proven that if I remain entwined with you, you will never disappoint me. Life with you is my greatest joy.

My Strength

You are my Strength and my Shield from every danger.
When I fully trust in you, help is on the way.
I jump for joy and burst forth with ecstatic, passionate praise!
I will sing songs of what you mean to me!

Psalm 28:7

I can't help but praise you! You're the God of mercy who rushes to my defense and saves me from danger. The way you answer my prayers amazes me. I don't know what I would do without you.

Yet it's more than the way you care for me; it's the fact that you call me your own and love me endlessly. Today, all I want to do is celebrate you. To dance and sing—passionately proclaim how much I love you.

Others pretend they don't want to know anything about you. They act as if they don't care about what you've done. But I know the truth—they only think that way because they've never encountered you. Everything would change for them if they would turn to you, even for a moment. You're a faithful Shepherd, always looking for those who have gone astray. Then you scoop them up in your arms and cherish them.

I pray that you would strengthen your people, so we never fall away from you, no matter what comes against us. Lord, I hold your name in highest regard and feast on the reality of your love.

God of Mercy

So hear me now, Lord; show me your famous mercy.
O God, be my Savior and rescue me!
Psalm 30:10

Lord, today I pause to reflect on your mercy, power, and grace. Forgive me for doubting; for taking your love for granted. I don't like the seasons when you seem far away. Panic grips my soul when my mind is occupied with the cares of this world. Darkness veils my eyes when I become prideful and expect what your grace so kindly provides.

Ever faithful, you broke through and poured out the mercy you are famous for. Though I became sick and depressed, you healed me. You turned my tears of sorrow into tears of joy. I've heard of what you've done for others, but now you've done it for me. I'm overcome, overwhelmed, and overjoyed by your unfailing love.

Thank you for not staying angry; for coming through for me time and time again. For recognizing my weakness and loving me anyway. Now, fully restored and wrapped in garments of glory, I'm alive again. I'm free, energized, and comforted by your life-giving presence.

All at Once

All at once the guilt of my sin washed away
and all my pain disappeared!

Psalm 32:5

Father, I've never known fulfillment and happiness quite like this. For so long I walked in pain and frustration, my soul devastated by the things I kept bottled up inside—the sin that separated me from you. But you wouldn't give up on me; you kept exposing my heart and offering me freedom. It wasn't until I refused to hide and finally acknowledged my sin that pain disappeared. All at once, the guilt and misery were completely gone!

This is what you do for us. This is why you lay your heavy hand of conviction upon our hearts—so we can be clean and experience true freedom. Let my life be a reflection of this ecstatic revelation. May the joy that continually spills from my lips ignite a spark of hope in others, so they will turn to you as well.

As long as I keep my eyes on you, you'll lead the way. As we walk together on the pathway of life, you'll instruct me and surround me with your love.

Creator

Now, with breathtaking wonder,
Let everyone worship Yahweh, this awe-inspiring Creator.
Psalm 33:8

Father, you inspire me. My being is filled to overflowing with declarations of praise. Melodies flow unceasingly from my lips. With words of life, you breathe clarity into the most obscure places, and I'm reminded over and over again how majestic you are.

You breathe light into the galaxies with stars too vast to number and illuminate my body with your Spirit. The same hands that are big enough to measure the oceans are careful enough to cradle me with love. You began the earth with words of promise and each one will come to pass.

You're forever faithful, unfailing in love; the Master Creator who gazes upon all he has made and declares it good. Yet nothing holds your heart the way we do. Even our weakest worship captures your attention. I feel you gazing at me from heaven, overshadowing me with the radiance of your presence and smiling at me with kindness and compassion. Never stop, Lord, for I am awestruck by your love.

The Joy of Life

Gaze upon him, join your life with his, and joy will come.
Your faces will glisten with glory.
You'll never wear that shame-face again.

Psalm 34:5

Father, I wonder if everyone can see my face glistening with glory. Or if they get tired of hearing over and over again how much you've blessed me. If I'm boasting, it's only because of what you've done; it's only to make you famous. It's impossible for me to stay quiet! I want to tell everyone how kind you are, so they may experience it for themselves.

Lord, I ask that those who hear me would listen. Really listen. I want them to know that when we join our lives to yours, joy comes. I want them to give you thanks for the beauty that fills each day. To know that when they turn and hide themselves in you, you'll never turn them away. Even the angels stoop down to hear their prayers.

When I drink freely of your pleasure and indulge in your goodness, I think of those who haven't yet experienced your joyous mercy. I want to shout, "Come to the One who passionately pursues you and worship him in awe and wonder! Discover the joy of life with him!"

Never Let Me Down

O Lord, fight for me! Harass the hecklers, accuse my accusers. ...
Let them be the ones to fail and fall into destruction!
And then my fears will dissolve into limitless joy;
my whole being will overflow with gladness
because of your mighty deliverance.

Psalm 35:1, 8–9

Lord, my heart grieves for those who have risen up against me. I've done nothing wrong, yet they accuse me falsely and gossip behind my back. They slander my name and tear me to shreds with their lies. Be my judge and try my heart. I'm burdened by this injustice and pray for them like family. But quite honestly, I'm overwhelmed and I need you.

Hide me behind your shield. Rise up as my Savior, my mighty God. Vindicate me! Then I will lift my head to see what I've always known deep in my heart—you've been here all along. You had no intention of forsaking me!

Fear dissolves into joy like I've never known, when you show yourself strong on my behalf. You know how I am—there's no way I can hold it in. I'm going to find the biggest crowd I can and tell them what you've done for me! When I worship in the sanctuary alongside my closest friends, we'll be the ones singing the loudest, celebrating all you've done. You will never let me down!

My Portion

*The godly ones will have a peaceful, prosperous future
with a happy ending.*

Psalm 37:37

No matter what happens, I will always have more than enough, because I have you, Lord. Even in times of disaster, you will take care of me. Your favor is toward me because I am your child. Write your ways upon my heart, so I may never stray. I've seen the path of the wicked—may I never step a foot on it.

I choose to follow you and walk in your righteous decrees. Give me your wisdom, that I may become one of your finest counselors, one whose words are right and trustworthy. As I continue to walk steadily in your ways, patiently trusting, you will promote me when the time is right.

You are my daily portion. My strength. My deliverer. My Savior. You will never desert me. My faith is in you, because I love you. All of the godly ones will have a peaceful, prosperous future. Our story has a happy ending.

Abiding

At each and every sunrise we will be thanking you
for your kindness and your love.
As the sun sets and all through the night,
we will keep proclaiming, "You are so faithful!"

Psalm 92:2

The sun pools through my open window—you have blessed us with another day. A smile alights my face and melodies rise from my heart. I join the singing birds who announce your kindness and faithfulness. Everything that stands contrary to peace yields to my praise that fills the air.

Pour the oil of your Spirit upon my soul. As I place all of my affection upon you, I will thrive in your heavenly courtyard. Teach me to abide faithfully in this place of full surrender, so that even in my old age, I will be strong and fresh, bearing fruit for all to savor.

As I meditate on the kindness of your love, I'm gloriously overcome with gratefulness. I want to spend my life uncovering your rich mystery, searching the depths of your reality, and peeling back the layers of your love, which is manifest in all you do. Yes, your ways are deep and glorious secrets whispered to the hearts of those who seek you.

Experience the Wonder

So go ahead everyone and shout out your praises with joy!
Break out of the box and let loose
with the most joyous sound of praise!

Psalm 98:4

Sometimes I act a bit foolish, but I can't help it. Your love is like fire in my bones, blazing its way through blood and marrow—there's no containing it! You never refrain from showing your love and faithfulness, so I won't hold back my praise. I'll dance with abandon! I don't care who sees. Then I'll sing the songs that flow from my heart—no matter who hears. Nothing will hold me back, not even my own pride.

Lord, when I see the oceans roaring their praise, the rivers and streams clapping their applause, and the mountains giving you a standing ovation, I can't help but notice that something's wrong. All of creation flows in unison to honor you and declare your wonders, but those who you created in your image can't seem to do the same.

Come and make things right again. Let everyone experience the wonders you're famous for. Let them taste your everlasting love. I'll be here, celebrating in advance!

Uniquely You

He listened to all the groaning of his people
longing to be free and set loose
the sons of death to experience life.

Psalm 102:20

No one intervenes the way you do, Lord. Your intervention is uniquely you. You not only deliver us from trouble, but use what could have destroyed us to make us stronger and teach us of your faithfulness. Just when I think I understand your ways, you stun me with your infinite power and unlimited authority.

Release the glory of your presence into the nations, answering their longing for true freedom, and they will never be the same. Even their leaders will be stunned by the fascinating way you answer prayer. Generations to come will read the testimonies of your faithfulness and declare your praise.

Our destinies are handcrafted in heaven—each of your children infused with rare and costly attributes. No one has been left out. Lord, I pray for those who have yet to discover the hidden treasures of life with you. Loosen them from the shackles of doubt and unbelief—let them come to know the matchless joy of experiencing you.

Treasures of Truth

Our days are so few, and our momentary beauty
so swiftly fades away!
Psalm 103:15

There's a depth of beauty much deeper than what we see. Its elegance and charm emanates from those who are filled with holy fervor. It is known by those who are touched by it, perceived by all who approach it. This is the type of beauty I desire—the one that radiates with the essence of who you are.

Lord, I surrender my fleeting desires for ordinary things. I want to live my life soaring on the wings of your great love. A life of holy contemplation and deep joy that is felt by those around me. Pour your kindness upon my life—let it overflow its banks and flood my soul. May I never reach for trinkets, but always grasp the treasures of truth.

It is your mercy and love that have made me great. A mercy that extends higher than the highest firmament. A love greater than the splendor of heaven. With you, the harshest deserts bloom and hardest of hearts become pliable. Draw me in and I will run with you forever.

While I Wait

God's promise to Joseph purged his character
until it was time for his dreams to come true.
Psalm 105:19

Songs of praise rise from my lips as I wait for the fulfillment of your promises. Close to my heart is every word you have spoken. Be with me as I journey through this life. Cover me with a cloud of your presence by day. Guide me through the night with your fire. As long as you're with me, I know that every commitment you've made will come to pass.

Exploding from my being are the testimonies of your miracles. Your wisdom is seen in all you do. Even in the waiting, you refine my character and teach me patience and trust. You oversee every aspect of my life and remind me of your love.

I seek the light of your face. I reach for your strength and won't lose hope. You're the source of my strength, the fountain of my joy. Help me not to wrestle with these seasons of transition. You're forever faithful—true to your word. There's a time for every dream to be fulfilled.

Enduring Faith

*They grumbled and found fault with everything
and closed their hearts to your voice.*

Psalm 106:25

Father, drown my doubts and fears with your love. I don't want to test the limits of your mercy like the Hebrews did. They took your miracles for granted. Impatience drove them mad—demanding that you satisfy their cravings, because they forgot about your awesome power. I wonder how many times I've allowed my circumstances to wear me down and cause me to doubt.

I want faith that endures. To be one of the ones that brings you joy, by trusting you. Sometimes I step away from freedom and end up enslaved to fear and anxiety. And yet you come—over and over—to rescue me from bondage, just as you did with them. You're so patient. You know how frail we are, how easily we fear and forget what you've done. Your mercy never ceases to amaze me.

Help me to recognize you in every season. To be thankful, regardless of what I face and to honor you with absolute trust.

Your Love Carries Me

How he satisfies the souls of thirsty ones
and fills the hungry with all that is good!
Psalm 107:9

Lord, you're so good to me! When I was broken and desperate, stumbling in a wilderness of misery, you were there. In my darkest season, when it seemed I was living in a nightmare, your light broke through. I was starving for something food could never satisfy. A thirst that only your living waters could quench ravaged my soul. Then you came. You descended the hidden stairway in the sky and illuminated my world with your love. You satisfied me with your goodness. You came alive in me!

Even now your love carries me. Your presence brightens every day. I will lift my hands in unconditional surrender and unceasing praise. My imperfection was swallowed by your perfection. Teach me the ways of wisdom, so I may multiply your miracles upon the earth. I will deliver the oppressed and silence the enemy's lies. I will sing my story of miraculous salvation for all the world to hear.

Your mercy remains. Thank you for calming the storms of life.

No Other Answer than You

The Lord our God has brought us his glory-light!
I offer him my life in joyous sacrifice.
Tied tightly to your altar I will bring you praise.
For you are the God of my life and I lift you high,
exalting you to the highest place.

Psalm 118:27–28

Look at what you've done for me! I remember a time when all I could do was fall prostrate before you, offering you nothing more than my tears. It felt as if you'd abandoned me and that life had been drained from my body. The only act of faith I could manage was two hands gripping your altar. And there I waited. There was no answer for me other than you.

Instead of rebuke, you offered me compassion. You scooped me up in your strong arms and breathed strength back into my being. You reminded me of your faithfulness in times past and that you would save me again. You understood my weakness. When I could finally stand again, you took me by the hand and led me forward with patience.

That season made me strong. It gave me a chance to know you as a living Savior and a faithful, powerful God. From the deepest depths of my heart, I know that you love me. You will never abandon me. You filled my heart with peace. Now I offer my life in joyous sacrifice.

Truly Alive

My body trembles in holy awe of you,
leaving me speechless.
Psalm 119:120

This is life—to be with you. To hear you. To see you. Living for the glory of your love. Your promise of blessing is gracious—more than anyone deserves. Your words drip like oil from your being. They are alive. They are true. Beautiful.

I dive into the reality of your presence. You are here. You are faithful. You grasp my hand and guide me beyond the fears that shackle my soul. You set me free. I love you.

My body trembles in holy awe. I find no discourse to convey what once consumed this troubled mind. Nothing else matters when I find the light of your face. I want your glory seeping into every crevice—leave no part of me untouched by your radiant love.

In you I have peace. In you I am truly alive. In you I will remain.

Thank You

When you sleep between sharpened stakes,
I see you sparkling like silver and glistening like gold,
covered by the beautiful wings of a dove!

Psalm 68:13

Thank you for the cross, Jesus. When I look into your eyes, I remember—no one loves me like you do. Your nail-scarred hands still hold me. With your stripes you healed every sickness. You suffered in my place and bore my shame. Forgiveness was offered for my every sin.

Though bloody and beaten, the Prince of heaven radiated with the pure, perfect beauty of undefiled love. What glory shone from a darkened, bloody cross! To think it was your passion for me that held you there is unfathomable. My cries of praise and words of thanks are not enough.

I offer you this humble life. Even that isn't my own—it was a gift from you. I will live in victory, rising above every opposition, just as you did when you rose from the dead. Pierce my opinions with your revelation truth, just as you were pierced at the place of the skull. Let your Holy Spirit flood me with eternal life, so rivers of living water will flow from the depths of my being.

King of my heart, you did it for me. The finished work of the cross—all for your bride.

Rest

Now I can say to myself and to all:
"Relax and rest, be confident and serene,
for the Lord rewards fully those who simply trust in him!"

Psalm 116:7

Lord, teach me to rest. When commitments and responsibilities begin to suck me dry, remind me you're my place of refreshing. Help me to take care of myself—spirit, soul, and body. To listen to the clues my body gives me when it needs to be tended to.

When my mind is running with a million different thoughts, I sit in the quiet of your presence and give you each notion. I turn my focus to the simplicity of loving you, and I trust you to tend to each matter. You're faithful to lead me to your presence, where peace overshadows every care.

Bless me with time—however much it takes—so I can find the stillness my soul desires. Meet with me, as I draw near to you, and soothe my frazzled nerves. When I'm restless and cannot hear your voice, I know you're still here. Teach me to listen for you in the countless other ways you speak. Remind me that as the seasons change, so do the means by which you manifest your love.

Messiah

Jehovah-God has taken a solemn oath
and will never back away from it, saying:
"You are a priest for eternity, my King of righteousness!"
Psalm 110:4

You are the Messiah, the profound mystery that sets our hearts ablaze. The lowly babe, sought by shepherds on that holy night, has become our King of righteousness. Now, as we behold your glory, the incomprehensible becomes comprehensible. With songs of angels and laughter that frees our soul, we celebrate your birth.

Light of the world, you penetrated the darkness and brought hope to our hearts. We bow before your majesty and pour out the fragrant offering of our love today and every day. Clothe us with your holy splendor and radiate through us for all the world to see. Consume us with the fire of your passionate love. We want to become your radiant bride who holds nothing back from you. May our lives be a gift that honors you.

Your Word Is Alive

Ineffable cravings and lovesick longings consume me
as I thirst for more revelation of your commands.

Psalm 119:131

I've fallen in love with you. Your words mean more to me than a vault filled with the purest gold. Your face shines upon me in brilliant glory. The path you have set before me is filled with promise. The motive for everything you do is pure—I want to be like you. I want to understand the mystery of your ways.

Break open your words within me so that your revelation shines forth. Let my speech be saturated with your wisdom, so that those with open hearts can feast upon it. Instruct me on what is right in your eyes, so that sin will never have dominion over me. Nothing is more pure and eternal than your truth. Your marvelous words are living miracles—tangible and alive. They satisfy the cravings of my soul. I'm gripped by a furious passion to follow them forever.

Identity

We have the privilege of worshiping the Lord, our God.
For he is our Creator and now we belong to him!
We are the people of his pleasure.
Psalm 100:3

Lord, help me to remember who you have created me to be. Never let me forget or get confused about my true identity. I am your child—a beautiful masterpiece with a glorious purpose. You delight in me.

You love me. I am never alone because you are with me. You have filled me with your Spirit, and I'm a vessel of purity and honor. I'm the extension of your love on this earth and will carry myself with compassion. I shine with the radiance of your glory—a light for the whole world to see. I'm beautiful just the way you made me.

I won't allow the world to dictate what I think about myself or what I believe. You've given me everything I need to live a happy and successful life. I'm clothed in favor, blessed with wisdom. I'm worthy to be treated with dignity and respect and will treat others the same way. You've blessed me with perfection—I'm a mirror image of you.

Learning to Love

You don't look at us only to find our faults, just so that you can hold a grudge against us. You may discipline us for our many sins, but never as much as we really deserve. Nor do you get even with us for what we've done.

Psalm 103:9–10

Thank you for your mercy. You're so gracious and forgiving; always reaching out to me even in my darkest hour of shame. You always believe the best about me and never focus on my faults. The way you love always draws me closer and never pushes me away.

Lord, give me the grace to be this way toward others. To look beyond their words and actions and remember we're all in need of your grace and mercy. Teach me to see others the way you see them. Show me the value each person has, even if I don't agree with how they live. Speak to me about the purposes you created them for, so I can treat them the same way you do. Help me to speak with dignity, respect, and compassion to everyone I meet. Let my words and my actions agree. May I never cast judgment on others when I don't know their hearts. May I never behave in a way that pushes people away, but always show kindness, the same way that you do.

Your forgiveness toward me is never-ending and I will extend that same mercy toward others. You never expect anything in return. You simply love, because that is who you are—and I was created to be just like you.

Creativity

Let the entire universe erupt with praise to God.
From nothing to something he spoke and created it all.
Psalm 148:5

Beautiful Creator, you astound me. I'm mesmerized by all you've made. You're the Master Artist of all creation. The stars are dancing in your honor and from the depths below, creatures we've never seen echo your praise. No one in heaven or earth could ever do what you've done.

You made us in your image and encourage us to emulate all you do—how exciting! Your many art forms come to life through us. You've given us such magnificent ways to bring beauty into this world—dance, drama, music, writing, art, media. The list is endless when we create with you. When we release the gifts you've given us, we fill the world with extensions of who you are. Just like you, we breathe life into the earth.

Lord, give me creative and fresh ideas that flow effortlessly. Open doors for me to use my gifts in ways that bless others. Teach me and anoint me, so that every execution of my craft will come forth with wisdom and skill. Let everything I release touch others' hearts and speak to the deepest part of who they are.

Bless My Business

If God's grace doesn't help the builders,
they will labor in vain to build a house.

Psalm 127:1

God, bless the work of my hands. May everything I do prosper and bring forth fruit. Give me wisdom, so that I don't waste time on worthless endeavors. Open doors of recognition, so that no venture ever goes unnoticed.

Whether starting my own business or running with ideas for witty inventions, I want everything I do to be done in a spirit of excellence. Even when I'm serving others, give me strength, creativity, and integrity, in order to serve them well.

Surround each project with favor, so word will spread about all I have to offer. Bless the marketing and draw the masses. Pour out the finances to put things into play. Give me creative ideas that will make my product or business even better, and give me wisdom in the implementation.

Anoint me with grace and ease. Teach me, so I become the best at what I do. Help me to hone my skills—take each undertaking from glory to glory. I submit them all to you.

Like You

Keep cleansing me, God,
and keep me from my secret, selfish sins;
may they never rule over me!
For only then will I be free from fault
and remain innocent of rebellion.

Psalm 19:13

Lord, you're the most generous person to ever have walked the earth. Everything you did, you did for a lost and dying world—even for those who despised you. You're the perfect example of unselfishness; the epitome of benevolence. I want to be like you.

Cleanse me from selfish sins; from self-seeking motives that only benefit me. If there is any place void of your glory in me, fill it with yourself. Teach me the way of agape love—a love that gives, expecting nothing in return. Let the same compassion that fills you fill me. I want to esteem others higher than myself. Open my eyes to see others the way that you do.

You're always thinking of ways to bless me. Give me creative ideas to do the same for others. Give me grace to step out of what feels comfortable to me and go the extra mile to serve others and pour out love. Beautiful Savior, I will follow after you.

About the Authors

Dr. Brian Simmons is known as a passionate lover of God and the lead translator of The Passion Translation, a new heart-level Bible translation that conveys God's passion for people and his world by translating the original, life-changing message of God's Word for modern readers. Brian and his wife, Candice, travel full-time as speakers and Bible teachers.

Gretchen Rodriguez is a writer and author of award-winning fiction. Her heart burns with one main message: intimacy with Jesus and discovering the reality of his presence. She is also a dancer and ballet teacher. She and her husband, along with their three daughters, invested nine years as missionaries in Puerto Rico, and now make Redding, California, their home.